Strategic Analysis and Choice

Strategic Analysis and Choice

A *Structured Approach*

Alfred G. Warner

Strategic Analysis and Choice: A Structured Approach
Copyright © Business Expert Press, LLC, 2010.

First published in 2010 by
Business Expert Press, LLC
222 East 46th Street, New York, NY 10017
www.businessexpertpress.com

ISBN-13: 978-160649-175-1 (paperback)

ISBN-13: 978-160649-176-8 (e-book)

DOI 10.4128/9781606491768

A publication in the Business Expert Press Strategic Management collection

Collection ISSN: 2150-9611 (print)
Collection ISSN: 2150-9646 (electronic)

Cover design by Jonathan Pennell
Interior design by Scribe, Inc.

First edition: October 2010

10 9 8 7 6 5 4 3 2 1

Printed in Taiwan

To my wife, Jonne

Abstract

Strategy and strategic planning at the firm level often gets a bad reputation because managers aren't trained in it, and the tools are unfamiliar, infrequently used, and often poorly applied. The outcomes of these efforts can therefore be incomplete, biased, and far too subjective—and the results disappointing. One purpose of this book is to overcome this problem of familiarity by developing a systematic approach to conducting a strategic analysis. From assessing the general industry environment to analyzing industry forces and firm resources, well-known models are introduced and explained. This culminates in selecting a strategy that is consistent with industry and firm specific conditions.

Another problem is that the entire strategic process might seem fruitless, especially if it is treated as an episodic or occasional task. If the result of all that work is a document that gets put on a shelf or in a closet, what is the point? The second purpose of this book is to develop the idea that strategic development is a broad based and ongoing process. Strategy may ultimately be the responsibility of the CEO but it needs, and benefits from, the engagement of others. Done right, that engagement and development aligns the organization more effectively. In addition, the models connect to and reinforce each other. To use them well requires reflection and revision. In short, the process is not ever completely done—analysis becomes a lens you constantly bring to bear on your firm and its environment.

Keywords

Strategy, industry analysis, resources, SWOT, cost leadership, differentiation, prospector

Contents

Preface

Strategic Analysis and Choice: A Structured Approach is intended to both complement course work in firm level strategy at the senior undergraduate, MBA, and executive educational levels and to stand alone as a resource for managers working through the strategic planning process outside the classroom. This book was written to address problems that students typically encounter in trying to apply some well-known tools to case and real world material. These tools are often presented in strategy textbooks at fairly abstract levels and while students understand that they are to do something, they don't really know how to go about it. Practical application of the concepts does not prove to be intuitive for many, and this has frustrated them—and me. Because of this, strategic analysis can get a bad reputation in the classroom and in the world as difficult, incomplete, and biased. When managers believe this, strategy gets reduced to a formality with no real potency or meaning.

I believe that this represents a significant missed opportunity. Good analysis is a window on the world; without it, decisions are guesses. From the analytics, strategic choice can powerfully unite and coordinate elements of the firm. These are desirable outcomes. Thus, my objective with this book is to make the concepts more concrete and easy to use for working managers and those who will become managers. As you'll see, the emphasis is on analytics and how to ask and answer questions that lead to stronger, more thoughtful and considered conclusions. No such work can be exhaustive as there are more factors and models than can be reasonably addressed in a brief work, but the principles are extendable to new analytic criteria. Analysis will still be hard work, but this book should provide a roadmap that makes it more tractable.

Many people have helped with this book, and I would like to acknowledge their efforts. First, my thanks to students in my undergraduate and graduate strategy courses at Pennsylvania State University-Erie for their insights into what I thought was clear but perhaps was not. In particular, I thank Renee Brunner, Diane Detar, Robert Gorzynski, and

Anna Smialek for their detailed discussions. I also thank my colleague Jim Fairbank for his comments on an early draft. I particularly thank my wife, Jonne, for her close reading and suggestions over several iterations, improving both writing clarity and managerial sensibility.

I also thank the editorial team at Business Expert Press. Mason Carpenter not only gave this idea a chance but made it comparatively easy and painless to carry through. Cindy Durand has been invaluable in guiding me through process pitfalls in finishing up the work.

CHAPTER 1

Strategy as Process and Product, or How to Build a Business Strategy Without Too Much Pain

Introduction

Every firm needs a strategy for competing and surviving (if not succeeding) in its market, and this is no less true for small shops than it is for large, diversified firms. Firms lacking strategy wander without direction, spending resources on initiatives and projects that often conflict with other firm efforts. Often spasmodically reacting to the latest crisis, they introduce products and services that imitate those of more successful firms—but weakly so, without the cachet or the cost efficiency of the leaders. Employees don't know the "right" thing to do and neither do managers. In short, firms without a strategy fail. Yet, strategic planning often gets a bad reputation because it doesn't seem to work. Actual business outcomes are often less than satisfactory, so strategic planning must be useless, right?

I argue that there are two major potential causes of these results: poor formulation or poor execution. In the latter case of poor execution, the strategy simply is not implemented properly. The best-crafted strategy, if not well *executed*, is a hollow product. Therefore, understanding gaps in implementation is a very useful and highly recommended exercise. However, in this book I focus on the primary and more fundamental cause: The strategy is not *crafted*, or developed, properly.

This can happen for a number of reasons. First, developing a strategic plan is often perceived to be difficult, time consuming, and sometimes just a self-congratulatory exercise. The tools strategists use are unfamiliar to many managers, and as they are infrequently—if ever—used, it is hardly surprising that participants are unhappy! Just as playing one round each year is a poor way to keep up golfing skills, inexperience and unfamiliarity leads to outcomes that are incomplete, biased, and far too subjective. One purpose of this book is to overcome the perceived problem of difficulty by developing a systematic approach to strategic analysis that makes the tools more familiar and accessible. I introduce and explain well-known models, from assessing the general industry environment and analyzing industry forces and firm resources. These models culminate in selecting a strategy that is consistent with industry and firm specific conditions.

Another problem is that the strategy process is treated as an episodic or, as described earlier, spasmodic task. Once crises emerge, the firm needs a new or improved strategy, but all that strategy work has to be done while the business still needs running—and that's hard! The second purpose of this book, then, is to help you see how to avoid the novelty trap through the perspective that strategy is not just a product or outcome but a process, if not a way of thinking. Strategy may ultimately be the responsibility of the CEO, but it needs (and benefits) from the engagement of others.[1] Done right, that engagement and development aligns the organization more effectively. In addition, the models we'll explore connect to and reinforce each other, and using them well requires reflection and revision. In short, strategy crafting is not ever completely done. This is a virtue because analysis becomes a lens you constantly bring to bear on your firm and its environment.

The outline of this book is as follows: In the remainder of this chapter, I will discuss some of the definitional problems regarding strategy and what we are trying to accomplish with it as well as cover some economic principles that are the logical basis for the models or frameworks we'll subsequently develop. Chapter 2 focuses on building a good beginning by developing a detailed and inclusive definition of the industry. Being thorough here prevents problems of too broad or too narrow an analytic scope, and it also gets you to ask and answer important questions about customers, products, and processes that will be used repeatedly. Chapter 3 introduces a process called PEST or PESTLE for systematically assessing what is happening in the general—that is, outside the industry—environment (see Figure 1.1).

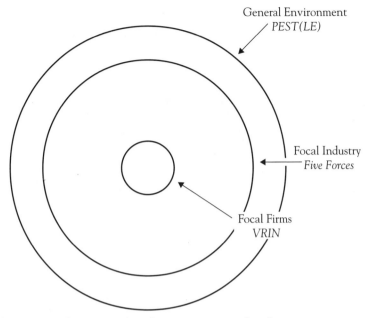

General Environment
PEST(LE)

Focal Industry
Five Forces

Focal Firms
VRIN

Figure 1.1. Competitive analysis: contexts and tools.

Chapters 4 and 5 introduce and elaborate Michael Porter's well-known Five Forces model of industry analysis as a way to understand the factors affecting the internal environment of a focal industry. Chapter 6 turns to understanding why, given the general environmental and industry characteristics you've uncovered, some firms perform better than others. The fundamental idea here is that resource differences are the source of performance differences, and you'll learn how Barney's VRIN model (which identifies resources that are Valuable, Rare, Inimitable, and Nonsubstitutable) can help you identify important resources. Since the purpose of all this is to craft a strategy, chapter 7 pulls this material together in an exploration of various conceptions of strategic approach. Different as they may appear to be from each other, there are some very important and clear similarities that should drive your approach. Chapter 8 addresses some criticisms and concerns about strategy in dynamic or rapidly changing environments, and chapter 9 concludes this book with reflections on and recommendations for making strategy a powerful tool for you and your firm.

What Is Strategy?

Probably, most people would answer the question of the definition of strategy with some statement about strategy as a plan, and this is, in fact, a pretty good start. However, it leaves a lot in the air as to content or structure or even objective. I think it is useful to begin by probing the roots of the word to get a better starting point.

Strategy derives from the Greek words *strategoi* and *strategos*, or "generals" and the "work of generals." That is, strategy was originally about what leaders did to win battles and wars. It is not hard to see how that idea gets extended to games or sports, like chess or football, or even to business because the objective is often perceived as the same—beating the competition. What is it that generals think about? What factors enter into their calculations and plans? What do they consider as they craft an approach to battle? At a basic level, generals must ask and answer questions about what resources they have, what resources the other side has, where the battle is to be fought, and the importance of the conflict at all (e.g., is it essential to fight here and now? Is it essential to win or only to delay?).

When generals consider resources, they might well begin by focusing on the soldiers available to them both in quantity and quality. Other considerations would include material assets (such as artillery, shot, shell, and transport) and supplies (such as food, water, and shelter). In short, the resource assessment tells a general something about what he can (but not should) do. Getting from "can" to "should" means that the same sort of analysis has to be conducted for the enemy forces. What resources do they have? What skills or assets are important to them? What is their supply situation? Finally, generals would consider the context of battle, the geography and climate or weather, as they decide when and where to fight.

For example, consider the Peninsular War or the conflict between France and England in Spain and Portugal in the early 1800s. Napoleon's French armies had swept through Europe with battle tactics that seemed unstoppable. At that time, opposing armies usually faced each other in lines, but Napoleon configured his forces to fight as narrow but long columns of soldiers. These could pierce the relatively shallow lines of opponents, and when this happened, the enemy force was not only divided and contained but the French troops could also bring fire against their enemies from the front and the rear. Still, the English went to battle against Napoleon's armies in line formation—and won. How?

In part, the answer lies in technology and training. Infantry was armed with smoothbore muskets. Smoothbores are not very accurate because of the round ball, lack of rifling, and the fact that soldiers often turned their heads or shut their eyes when they pulled the trigger to avoid powder burns. Beyond 50 yards, hitting anything was a matter of luck. What all generals realized was that a mass of infantry with muskets was still a formidable force—at least, until Napoleon arrived—because the simultaneous firing by thousands of soldiers put enough bullets in the air to make probability work in their favor. In other words, enough bullets would hit to damage the enemy. A drawback to the musket, though, was that it took a long time to reload because the gun needed powder, wadding, ball or bullet, more wadding, and priming before it could be fired again. In general, soldiers might be able to fire as a group (essential to this sort of battle) twice a minute. This was Napoleon's insight: Given a two per minute firing rate, if the French columns could move fast enough, then the losses from enemy fire would not be sufficiently high enough to prevent breakthrough and victory.

The English army was different, though. More than any other, it had institutionalized, or standardized, training for soldiers, particularly in musketry. English soldiers drilled and drilled until a company could generate a fire rate of three, four, or perhaps even five shots per minute. Imagine what sort of difference this makes to an approaching column; the first volley from a broad line directed at both sides of the column would be expected, but because reloading was so rapid, the subsequent volley fire by the platoon would mean a continuous ripple of shot. The French would have no respite from the fire and losses would be much higher than expected, high enough to slow the column down. And, once slowed (then stopped), the column was virtually defenseless as few soldiers could return fire. Thus, a consideration for English generals was to offset enemy strengths (columns) by deploying key resources (trained musketry) appropriately (where lines could be deployed—i.e., broad battlefronts).

Two confrontations with the French during the 1810 Portugal campaign illustrate the English strategic approach. Napoleon's armies had swept Spain, deposed the king, and only Portugal remained as a holdout on the peninsula. The British army under Sir Arthur Wellesley (later Lord

Wellington) was just hanging on; in fact, if Napoleon's General Masséna had been successful in pushing the English out of Portugal, then it would have become virtually impossible to confront Napoleon in Europe. In September of 1810, Masséna was marching toward Lisbon for a final battle. He was anxious to end the campaign as winter was coming and Napoleon's armies did not depend on provisioning from headquarters but on local supply. Capturing Lisbon was critical.

Wellington adopted two plans. The first was to intercept and to battle the French on the way to Lisbon at a place called Bussaco. The second, and far more ambitious plan, was called the Lines of Torres Vedras. At Bussaco, on September 27, 1810, Wellington and elements of the British and Portuguese armies had occupied the top of a long ridge while the French had camped in the valley below. Masséna believed that the French had to get over the ridge to proceed to Lisbon but by ceding the high ground to the British and Portuguese, he faced an almost impossible task. Indeed, marching columns up a steep slope would slow them (eliminating the power of speed) and leave them exposed to the murderous infantry fire described earlier. Nonetheless, Masséna attacked. The French suffered 4,600 casualties that day to the British-Portuguese's 1,252[2] and did not take the ridge. On the next day, the French cavalry discovered a road that would avoid the ridge altogether so Masséna moved on toward Lisbon, and the British abandoned the ridge and moved to intercept at Torres Vedras.

Observe how important terrain is to enhancing or degrading assets. The slope of the hill helped nullify the rapid striking power of the French columns. Terrain plays an even more critical role in the next meeting two weeks after Bussaco. In 1809, Wellington had commanded the development of the most ambitious earthworks ever created as the ultimate defense of Lisbon. The Lines of Torres Vedras were a series of interlocking forts and cannons along *30 miles* of two parallel ridges that stretched from the Atlantic Ocean to the Tagus River. Moreover, the engineers of the British Army had enhanced the natural geography by blasting hillsides into small cliffs all along the ridges, flooding the interior valley, eliminating any natural cover, and developing support roads behind the lines to move troops. Masséna and the French staff quickly recognized—after one attack—that any attempt to force Torres Vedras was hopeless, and they were forced to retreat. This was of great significance in the war: Winter was coming; there were no supplies to be had; and because Lisbon was unreachable, the French Army would be severely degraded by disease and hunger. Moreover, the British had secured a foothold on the Peninsula and from that could support campaigns in the coming years. It was the turning point of the war.[3]

The defenses of Torres Vedras are excellent examples of strategic thinking, even though there was no real battle fought here. Wellington struck very effectively at Napoleon's logistic weakness, crippling an army required to live off the land. This illustrates that the objective of military strategy is to win the war, not a battle. Thus, Bussaco was a win but not terribly important other than it stung and delayed the French. Torres Vedras was the great win, even though no real battle was fought.

So how do these examples relate to managers and business? In one sense, the process maps completely. As managers, you should also analyze environment, opposition, and resources, and from that analysis, construct strategies that exploit opportunities or negate threats (see Figure 1.2). Probably every CEO believes that he or she has a strategy for the firm, even if others crafted it. Still, most firms are not very successful (if success is defined as outperforming others in the industry). One of the key issues is the value of that strategy—that is, what went into developing it? Generals don't get to be generals

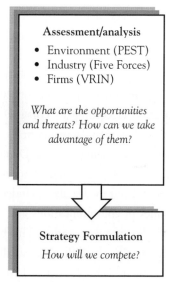

Figure 1.2. The strategy cycle (part 1).

without a substantial amount of disciplined training in military history, and strategy, but the same may not be true for managers. The benefit of training in strategic thinking is that developing a good plan is much more likely to happen if your thinking is disciplined, formal, and based on good theories or models. Yet, managers often fail at this, and their plans don't work out.

Clayton Christensen and Michael Raynor[4] argue that a large part of the problem is the willingness of managers to adopt recommendations from the seemingly endless flow of consultants or gurus (just look at the business shelves at any bookstore) without careful critical thought about the merits of the advice. There is no doubt that some of these books work—sometimes—but where is a manager to begin? In this book, we focus on understanding some particularly well-known and widely applied models or theories of competition; we learn how to apply them; and we draw conclusions in a very structured way.

Strategy as Process

Wellington was good, no doubt, but even he suffered setbacks. The old saying that no battle plan survives contact with the enemy (that's why they are called the enemy!) is illustrative and shows the limitation of plans. In other words, if success depends on everything going exactly as planned, failure is almost certain. Earlier, I noted that most firms don't succeed. The problem gets worse: Even successful firms have profound difficulty maintaining industry leading performance over time. For example, the shifts in the membership of the top 20 firms in the United States from 1958 to 2008 (according to Fortune) are illustrative. The 1958 version is dominated by manufacturing firms, such as the big three automakers, Bethlehem Steel, Boeing, General Dynamics, and, of course, seven oil companies.[5] By 2008, the list had changed quite dramatically.[6] Wal-Mart was number one, but the list also included six financial institutions and five companies in communications and computers. Only six firms repeated from the list fifty years earlier. This happened to the largest, most robust firms; imagine the difficulties smaller firms face in contending with seismic shifts in technology, social structure, regulation, or political economies and trade policy.

Often, part of the problem lies in how managers regard their planning. When crafting strategy is regarded as just a formality, the work gets put on the shelf somewhere and managers work on instinct, hunches, and whatever fire burns brightest on the desk. They are, as we'll see later, strategic reactors. A better position, although still problematic, is one that regards the strategy making process as only an analytic tool. As Montgomery[7] points out, though, really effective strategies are dynamic and adaptive (meaning they change to fit new circumstances and conditions). This is, as Figure 1.3 illustrates, the role of assessment, or measuring how well the strategy is working. Good assessment leads to feedback and reconsideration of the analysis and assumptions made earlier (as these are virtually always not quite right). This cycle should lead to a refined view and a better plan.

Moreover, assessment also highlights the purpose or vision of the firm. Montgomery quotes John Browne, former CEO of British Petroleum to this end, "Our purpose is who we are and what makes us distinctive. It's what we as a company exists to achieve, and what we are willing and not willing to do to achieve it." Thinking effectively about the world enables managers to recraft, clarify, strengthen, and reinforce vision and purpose.

Therefore, effective strategy making is not just a one-off analytic exercise but a *way of thinking* about your firm and the environment and industry in which it operates. Strategy becomes a living document and strategic thinking a disciplined way of viewing the world.

Some Economic Background for Competitive Analysis

Since strategy is about understanding firm performance and competitive advantage, it will be useful to review some fundamental microeconomic concepts about industries, firms, and performance and connect them to the work we'll be doing later.

When a firm has a competitive advantage, we should expect it to show up in performance, and it is reasonable to expect that that performance will be better than its competitors. Firm performance has been measured in many ways. In particularly volatile industries, for example, survival can be a useful measure. More broadly, researchers have measured outcomes like growth in market share or revenue, improvements in efficiency, stock price, liquidity,

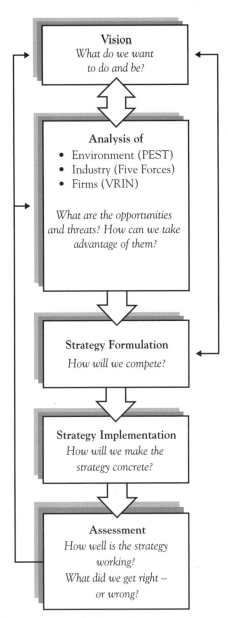

Figure 1.3. The strategy cycle (part 2).

and so on, but the most popular measure is some version of profitability.[8] We'll use this as our departure point and define competitive advantage as *abnormal profitability*, or profitability greater than the industry average.

To be more specific, we are interested in profitability measured a certain way. Just using profit dollars as a measure is not a good choice as it tends to make large firms better than small firms just because they are large. What we need is a measure that corrects for size differences and tells us something useful about how efficient a firm is at turning revenues into profits. What would really be a good measure is a comparison of the firm's weighted average cost of capital (WACC) versus its return on invested capital (ROIC). This can be calculated, but it is cumbersome; we are going to rely on a proxy for this and use profit margins (either gross or net—and sometimes both). The reason this proxy is useful is based in some fundamental microeconomic ideas about industries.

Economists can analyze what happens in industry competition and how equilibrium is reached by making some simplifying assumptions about industry structure and the firms in them. For example, in the simplest models industry entry and exit are assumed to be costless (i.e., firms can freely come and go). Similarly, firms are assumed to have the same technologies (i.e., firms do not differ in the products they offer) and to be price takers (i.e., consumers are price driven). Finally, firms are assumed to be too small to greatly affect supply individually. With these assumptions in hand, economists show that the equilibrium profitability for any industry is . . . zero!

That bears a little explanation. Let us first understand the difference between economic and accounting profits. We are all familiar with accounting profits, or revenues less costs. If the costs we take out are just the immediate costs of production (COGS), we have gross profit. If we also take out administrative and other indirect costs, we end up with net profit—but in either event, profit equals revenues minus costs. Economic profit includes the opportunity cost of being in the industry (that is, the return an investor would expect) in the equation. Some industries are safe and stable while others are volatile and risky. The return or opportunity cost should reflect this. The economic return is calculated as accounting profit less opportunity cost. That is, from an economist's perspective, if a firm or investor got a return exactly equal to the opportunity cost, economic profits would be zero.

Let's see how this conclusion develops. Figure 1.4 shows the supply curve of an individual firm where AC = Average Cost and MC = Marginal

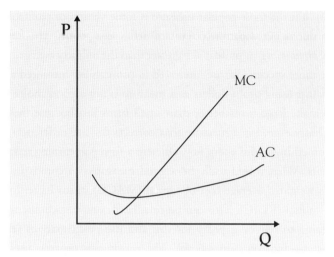

Figure 1.4. Individual firm supply curve.

Cost. The short hand description here is that firms are willing to supply product where the *MC* > *AC* because the price paid for any such quantity (the vertical axis) is greater than the average cost to produce them. Economists also show that industry supply is additive; if another firm joins the industry, we'll see the supply curve shift to the right.

In Figure 1.5, we see an industry with a single firm where LRAC means long run average cost (which proxies, or stands in, for the opportunity cost). What can you determine about the profitability of the firm? Is profitability greater than the opportunity cost? If so, and the conditions about firm entry and exit described earlier hold, what would you expect to happen? You should expect that other firms and investors would see this as abnormal profitability and would want to enter. Assume one does enter, what happens? Figure 1.6 demonstrates the additive nature of supply as the supply curve shifts to the right. What happens to profits? Is the industry still attractive?

It turns out we can continue this process until the supply curve shifts to intersect demand and the LRAC simultaneously. When that happens, profits are equal to cost (particularly opportunity costs) so economic profits equal zero. It is essential to note that this will happen *every time in every industry* if the assumptions described earlier hold or are true. Yet, we know that firms don't always perform the same and that some firms are

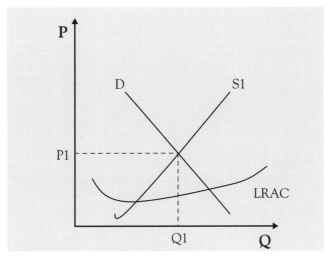

Figure 1.5. A single-firm industry.

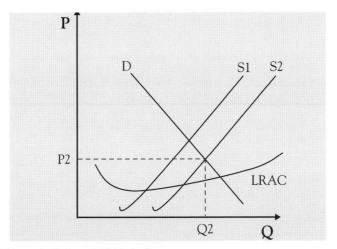

Figure 1.6. A multifirm industry.

more profitable than others. That's why we are in business! The problem, then, is to figure out why and how these conditions don't hold true and why some firms can take advantage of that to achieve abnormal profitability. As you'll see, both the industry analysis and firm analysis models reject some of the economic assumptions on very good grounds—and by doing so, generate powerful ways to explain what is really happening.

CHAPTER 2

Setting the Scope of Analysis

Defining Your Industry

Introduction

In this chapter you'll develop techniques for generating a thoughtful definition of the industry in which your firm competes. The idea of defining an industry and its boundaries may seem odd or maybe even pointless. After all, newspapers and television newscasters and politicians and all the rest of us are quite comfortable talking about the pharmaceutical industry or the auto industry or the air carrier industry. What needs to be defined?

In fact, though, *there is no such thing as an industry other than what we think it is!* Defining an industry is a conscious selection of a set of firms from a larger environment, so if we each have a different mental set that includes some firms and excludes other firms, then we have different definitions of what the industry really is. This will affect every subsequent step of the analyses you'll do in this book. For example, the U.S. air carrier industry might be defined as the largest carriers, such as Delta, American, United, US Airways, Continental, Southwest, and JetBlue. This list has the advantage of being short and capturing the largest of the competitors. Another approach would use the membership list of an industry association like the Air Transport Association. This is a broader list but the members are self-selected, which raises concerns about who might not have elected to join hence the inclusiveness of the list. The list includes firms of very different sizes and also includes UPS and FedEx as members. If you are interested in airfreight, this makes sense, but if you are interested in the firms that fly people, this is not an intrinsically good set. We might turn to the Bureau of Transportation Statistics, which reports on all passenger carriers with more than $20 million in annual revenue (of which there are 16 for 2009). The complete list of passenger carriers runs to 52. Deciding which is the *right* list (or, indeed, if another list is better) depends on the answers you derive to questions about the problems buyers are trying to solve when they make a purchase, the products or services that meet those buyers needs, and the firms that can provide the products or services.

So, why should you develop an industry definition? Given what you just read, it is possible to configure the carrier industry in many ways. One of the most common problems I've seen managers have as they learn this process is letting the scope of the industry change over the course of the analysis, which renders any conclusions suspect. Committing to one definition of industry at the outset drives a stake in the ground and keeps your analysis consistent. A second reason to develop an industry definition is because the questions you'll answer in developing a definition are used repeatedly in subsequent stages of the analysis.

Problems in Defining an Industry

In economics, an industry is often defined as the set of firms that provide close substitutes. In real life, managers often generate an industry definition (i.e., name the set of competitors) based on the competitive pressures they face at the time.[1] That is, what and for whom a firm produces now is the basis for determining how its managers will define competitors. For example, managers tend to classify firms as close competitors if they are similar in form and if they share and compete for the same scarce resources, such as customers and suppliers. Typically, this is a subset of a larger set of firms that serve related/similar/connected markets. Managers can also make mistakes in populating their industry definition by focusing on the largest and best known firms while ignoring new or small or evolving firms.[2] These classifications are considered faulty or inferior because of a bias in judgment that comes about because search costs (i.e., really digging into the definition) are viewed as high. Perceived similarities with other firms make evaluation and assessment relatively easy and cost effective (in the sense that similar firms should respond or act similarly). Also, because industries tend to generate and participate in a commonly held knowledge trajectory,[3] firms may regard as competitors those firms that also share in or generate industry level knowledge in pursuit of solving the economically interesting problem. That is, these are firms that know and value the same things.

The rise of Wal-Mart serves as an example of the cognitive problems rivals might have had in deciding if Wal-Mart was really a competitor (at least, early on!). In the discount-retail industry of the 1950s and '60s, senior managers believed that a population base of 100,000 was needed to support the large scale, low-margin structure of the stores. Therefore, serious competitors sited stores in urban and suburban areas. However, Wal-Mart originated in small towns, serving broad rural areas that could tap 100,000 people who found themselves closer to a Wal-Mart store than a city-based discounter. That is, for firms in the discount retail industry, Wal-Mart might have differed too much in service area, if not in product or service (and, early on, was too small), to be considered as a competitor. Wal-Mart didn't hit Kmart, Bradlees, Caldor, Shopko, or other discount retailers as an obvious or important threat until years too late—after Sam Walton was well on his way to solidifying the foundations of industry-leading IT and logistic competence.[4]

Similarly, mistakes occur when managers fail to account for evolutionary—or even revolutionary—changes in the competition or product/service. In the book-selling industry, for example, until the 1960s or '70s, books were sold primarily through independent, local stores. These were typically small and urban. Moreover, they usually had a narrow focus such as used books or were limited to a specific discipline (like law) or genre (such as mysteries). Managers then might define the relevant industry as bookstores reasonably close to their physical location. Then, in the '60s, chain bookstores, such as B. Dalton, Waldenbooks, and Crown, emerged as mall-based, suburban stores. They were still small, convenience destinations (on the order of 5,000 sq. ft.), but because shopping patterns migrated away from urban to suburban and from private shops to malls, these firms drove many single stores out of business. Also, the scope of competition changed: The chain stores had national presence and, as we'll see, some associated strengths.

In the mid-eighties, both Borders Books and Barnes and Noble began to expand retail operations with a new model—the bookstore as a superstore and a destination. These were like other specialty, category-killer stores in that they were large (30,000 sq. ft.), offered a wide selection often at lower prices, and were stand-alone rather than mall-based (or they worked as an anchor). They also came to offer amenities, such as coffee bars, comfortable seating, and a relaxed environment. These damaged and eventually absorbed the mall-based chains. Finally, in the mid-nineties, the emergence of the Internet made new, virtual firms, such as Amazon and Alibris feasible.

Book retailers who failed to keep up with changes in shopping patterns and preferences, changes in the product or service being delivered or how it was delivered, or the competitors that emerged to take advantage of those changes were in trouble. Changes in the shape of the industry change the dynamics of competition. So, how can managers develop and maintain a better sense of what the industry is?

A Systematic Approach to Industry Definition

Previously I mentioned that the standard economic definition of industry is the firms that produce close substitutes. In strategy, and particularly in industry analysis, the word *substitutes* has a very specific meaning that differs from the standard economic definition, so I recommend the following definition of industry:

> An industry is the set of firms that solves the same economic problem in the same way.

How do we determine this set of firms? Clearly, just picking competitors without a rationale for inclusion or exclusion can yield very different outcomes. For example, when graduate students are asked to define the U.S. auto industry, several ad hoc approaches usually emerge. One is to name the firms headquartered in the United States (like GM, Ford, and Chrysler). The second is to focus on firms that manufacture in the United States (which adds Toyota, Honda, and BMW, among others). An extension adds all firms that sell cars in the United States. Finally, almost always, a definition pops up that includes not only firms that manufacture cars but also suppliers and firms involved in sales and financing (e.g., identifying seat or steering system manufacturers or dealerships as parts of the industry).

In fact, all are legitimate ways of starting the definition, and the latter approach anticipates a key analytic tool: the extended value chain. Still, lumping suppliers and buyers in the auto industry is almost always too large and diffuse a group, and focusing on only the largest firms may be shortsighted.

This is why we start with "solving" an "economic problem" and doing so "in the same way" across the industry firms. It helps you more completely define who the customers are (since they have the problem that needs or wants solving). It is also useful to be clear about how the problem is solved with respect to product or service characteristics and how those are produced. This approach can help develop stronger criteria for selection. More formally, the process requires the following actions:

- defining the key economic problem
  - Who are the ultimate consumers?
  - What is their problem or need?
  - How is the problem solved? (Product/service characteristics)
- naming the firms that solve this problem

We can use the U.S. auto industry as an initial example. To begin, we are interested in developing the boundaries of the industry or the firms we'll include or exclude. As a first pass, we know the industry firms produce cars. Who are the ultimate consumers of cars (i.e., the product of this industry)? The answer is usually individuals but also governments and rental fleets. Note that if it is not already specified in the problem, you will want to be clear about the scope of your consumer set. For instance, are you considering only the U.S. market or a more global one?

Second, what is the problem these consumers are trying to solve? This can be difficult to define because there are usually multiple facets; consumers are often trying to solve a number of interrelated problems simultaneously. It is very important and useful to understand these consumer preference profiles for several reasons. First, they will help develop the boundary of potential solutions. Second, they help identify potential (and powerful) substitutes. Third, they might lead you to customers who are not very satisfied with the industry solution but don't have many better choices, and these can be valuable new markets.

In this case, at the most basic level, consumers of cars want convenient transportation—and convenience might be defined as transportation when and where needed (i.e., personal and private, regardless of weather). We should flesh this out to establish when and why consumers may prefer autos rather than public transportation or other modes (such as bicycles). After that, needs or desires within the solution set vary. For example, if I were in the market for a new vehicle, I would have a number of problems or preferences I would want to address and I would want to maximize my satisfaction (my utility) in doing so. I drive 20 miles one way to school, and since it snows six months of the year where I live, a vehicle with all-wheel drive would be a good idea. On the other hand, 20 miles of driving and high gas prices make efficiency a key concern. I also like to haul material for gardens or fishing; a vehicle that has hauling capacity is a good idea. I also like to be comfortable, if not a little pampered, as I drive. Finally, I have a limited budget. This is a difficult set of preferences to satisfy (in one vehicle, anyway!) because they are internally not very consistent. For instance, all-wheel drive and fuel efficiency don't usually go together very well. Nor, usually, does hauling capacity and efficiency or luxury. Obviously, I'll have to weight some factors more heavily than others. Even if I do, though, changing external conditions can change how the factors are weighted. If gas prices spike or collapse, for example, the importance of efficiency will rise and fall.

What makes this interesting is that almost all consumers share most or all these concerns but to varying degrees, which is why industry offerings can be far more limited than the number of customers. Preferences are not usually driven by a single need but by many needs, and they often shift over time or as conditions change. Preferences are typically multidimensional; it is key to get a grip on what the major elements may be.

Understanding what consumers are trying to solve with their choices helps us determine the firms that can meet those needs. In a general sense, firms in the auto industry meet consumer preferences in the same way by offering one version or another of a self-contained, gasoline fueled, internal combustion driven machine in about the same size. A Yukon is bigger than a Cobalt, but they are within an order of magnitude (factor of 10) in size. This differs from, say, passenger planes where the smallest may carry four or five and the largest may carry a hundred times that many. In other words, the firms in the auto industry have solved the primary need of personal, private, and convenient transportation in a particular fashion. Preferences are met by the range of products offered or option packages.

This definitional process is important because it gives us guidance about the sorts of solutions that fit and those that don't. Are motorcycles equivalent solutions? Bicycles? Trucks? It would not be useful to include motorcycle-making firms as part of the industry because motorcycles solve the transportation problem in a different way, though not as differently as bicycles solve it. Still, there could be some crossover firms in this because Honda, Suzuki, and BMW make motorcycles and also make cars. We'll have to include these firms but only as auto manufacturing firms. Trucks are even trickier. Probably most people would include light trucks as part of the solution set (such as the Ford Ranger or Ford F150) but how about larger trucks? Are trucks like the Ford F350 the same sort of solution? Are semitrucks, such as Peterbilts or Freightliners or Macks, solutions (and their manufacturers part of the auto industry)? Probably not, but firms like Volvo and Daimler do participate in that large-truck industry. Again, we'll have to discriminate carefully.

Another part of understanding how the consumer problem is solved entails thinking about how industry products or services are actually produced and delivered. In some industries the same basic technologies are used by all competitors but in others they can range from fundamentally manual processes to highly automated and capital intensive ones (the furniture industry is a good example where you might include firms ranging from individual craft workers to the largest of the commodity manufacturers). This might make a difference in making sure the same sets of customers are being addressed. On the delivery side, consider the book retailer examples used earlier where products can come from both brick-and-mortar stores or from online retailers.

With needs identified and the product or service clarified, we can build a set of firms that comprises the industry. Table 2.1 lists the top

Table 2.1. Global Top 10 Auto Manufacturers H1 2009

1.	Toyota
2.	GM
3.	Volkswagen
4.	Hyundai-Kia
5.	Ford
6.	Peugeot-Citroen
7.	Honda
8.	Nissan
9.	Suzuki
10.	Renault

10 firms in global sales for the first half of 2009,[5] but since we are interested in the U.S. market, this might not be completely useful, as Citroen and Renault are not sold in the United States. Moreover, the relative sizes of the rest of the firms differ at the national level versus the global level. Table 2.2 lists the top 10 auto manufacturers in U.S. sales for 2009 according to the website Ward's Auto;[6] note the differences.

Alternatively Edmunds.com, a well-known car pricing and review site, has its own list of auto labels[7] (see Table 2.3), and Fiat, Peugeot, or Renault are not listed (though this may change with Fiat's investment in Chrysler). The list has no rank ordering, which makes it less useful than a top 10 list, but it is more inclusive. On the other hand, this list treats brands as individual entities rather than as components of a larger firm (e.g., Toyota and Lexus or General Motors and its then subsidiaries Saab, Saturn, and Hummer). It will take more research to define firms.

This gives rise to another issue: How many firms are enough to constitute a good definition of the industry? Looking ahead, you'll want your list to be tractable with members that have enough in common so that general environmental and industry analytics are workable. Too narrow a list means you run the risk of overlooking important small or emerging firms, but too broad a list makes managing the analysis much more complex. One approach is to keep the level of industry concentration in mind. Concentration refers to the extent to which industry revenues are controlled by just a few firms (very concentrated) or are broadly spread among many firms (not concentrated). A short list is more reasonable

Table 2.2. U.S. Top 10 Auto Manufacturers, 2009 (use Ward's auto)

1.	GM
2.	Toyota
3.	Ford
4.	Honda
5.	Chrysler
6.	Nissan
7.	Hyundai
8.	Kia
9.	Volkswagen
10.	Daimler

Table 2.3. Edmunds.com List of Manufacturers of New Cars

Acura	Chevrolet	Hyundai	Lincoln	Mitsubishi	Smart
Aston Martin	Chrysler	Infiniti	Lotus	Nissan	Spyker
Audi	Dodge	Jaguar	Maserati	Pontiac	Subaru
Bentley	Ferrari	Jeep	Maybach	Porsche	Suzuki
BMW	Ford	Kia	Mazda	Rolls-Royce	Tesla
Bugatti	GMC	Lamborghini	Mercedes-Benz	Saab	Toyota
Buick	Honda	Land Rover	Mercury	Saturn	Volkswagen
Cadillac	Hummer	Lexus	Mini	Scion	Volvo

in highly concentrated industries. For information on how to calculate concentration, see the appendix to chapter 5.

A rule of thumb to finish the list would be to rank the firms by size (unit output or revenues), and include the firms that contribute to the top 80% of sales. If, at the end of the process, you find many firms of the same size, you might include them as well.

As an illustration, we can apply this technique to the brewing industry, which has exhibited significant changes in concentration over time. The list of the top 10 brewers in 1950 (shown in Table 2.4)[8] indicates that the market was pretty evenly divided among these competitors. (Note that the largest brewer was barely twice the size of the seventh

Table 2.4. American Brewing Industry Top 10, 1950

Rank	Brewer	Share (%)
1	Jos. Schlitz Brewing	6.08
2	Anheuser-Busch	5.83
3	Ballantine, Inc.	5.22
4	Pabst Brewing Co.	4.90
5	Schaefer Brewing	3.16
6	Falstaff Brewing	2.73
7	Miller Brewing	2.51
8	Hamm Brewing	1.26
9	Genesee	0.81
10	Coors	0.80

largest. Moreover, the top 10 accounted for 33.3% of the market.) An industry definition would surely have to include all these firms and perhaps even more. Contrast that list with the distribution of sales in 2005 (see Table 2.5).[9] In the latter case, the industry is clearly dominated by three firms, which account for about 80% of market sales. Under some circumstances, this may be enough to use as a basis; though, note that if you were interested in the craft brewing segment of this industry, you would have a different set of firms to use, which would be led by many of the bottom six here.

As you consider candidate firms, you'll likely conclude that some are clearly on the list, some are clearly not, and some are difficult to classify. As a starting point, use the "clearly in" firms for the first passes at analysis, but don't forget the "maybe" firms. Later, you can add them to the analysis to see if they make any difference. The important concept to grasp is that just making a list without understanding the assumptions and limitations can skew and distort your list of industry members and damage your subsequent hard work.

There are a number of sources for information on what firms might constitute an industry. Obviously, for the auto industry, you've already seen data from Hoover's, Inc., a reputable source of industry and business data. Similarly, Dun and Bradstreet and Standard and Poor have industry profiles available at most libraries and online. You can also turn to industry associations for information. Most industries have an organization that stands in

Table 2.5. American Brewing Industry Top 10, 2005

Rank	Brewer	Share (%)
1	Anheuser-Busch	49.5
2	Miller Brewing	18.7
3	Molson-Coors Co.	11.1
4	Pabst Brewing	3.4
5	Yuengling and Son	0.8
6	Boston Beer	0.7
7	City Brewery	0.5
8	Latrobe Brewing	0.5
9	High Falls Brewing	0.3
10	Sierra Nevada	0.3

as a formal and collective voice on industry issues to others. In the auto industry, for example, there are groups such as the Association of International Automobile Manufacturers (AIAM) or the European Automobile Manufacturers Association (ACEA) or the Automotive Industry Action Group (AIAG), among others. Industry associations are a great source of material on issues beyond membership, too, because there is almost always some discussion of key issues facing industry firms. The brewing industry has its own associations including the Beer Institute, which covers the industry in general, and the Brewers' Association, which is more focused on the craft brew part of the industry. You might also search government websites, especially those of regulatory agencies. The auto industry, for example, is affected by work from the Department of Transportation (DOT) or the National Highway Traffic Safety Administration (NHTSA).

What is the right list of firms? That is up to you and the problem you are trying to analyze. In a political discussion, the U.S. auto industry might reasonably be construed as just the Big Three of Ford, GM, and Chrysler. As we've seen earlier, other lists vary with the question: should we include U.S.-based firms, firms that manufacture in the United States, or firms that sell in the United States? The right list depends on what you want to accomplish. What makes it right is that it is consistent with what you want to analyze, it is well defined, and it is inclusive.

Summary

Defining the industry is a useful, if not essential, beginning to competitive analysis. It compels us to think about customers, their needs or problems, and how some firms have elected to meet those needs. Being thoughtful about definition forces us to decide which firms are in and which firms are out. As you go forward through the analytic process, you'll likely find that your set of competitors (the industry) changes. That's usually because some decisions you make here in definition were explicitly or implicitly revisited and reassessed. Just make your sure you are aware of what changed in your thinking and why.

CHAPTER 3

Analyzing the General Environment

PEST or PESTLE Assessment

Introduction

A common and useful beginning to strategic analysis is to consider and assess the general or macroenvironment in which industries and firms operate. Here we are concerned with very large trends and movements that likely will affect the competitive position of firms and their success. In a sense, these are the ground rules of competition. Still, assessing the general environment seems like a very large and amorphous problem. How can you be sure that you are not overlooking the right information?

In chapter 2, you asked and answered questions about your industry. Here, you will address questions and find answers that define key issues for your industry. These are schema or models or ways of organizing information. The model we'll use in this chapter has been presented under a variety of names, but they all express the same idea: Getting a solid understanding of these issues is more easily done if you have an organized and thorough set of questions to ask and answer.

You will need to ask and answer questions about either four or six dimensions of the general environment. You will want to understand what effect **P**olitical, **E**conomic, **S**ociocultural, and **T**echnological factors will have on your industry's future. Note the topics—this arrangement is why the model is called PEST. The PESTLE approach simply separates **L**egal and **E**nvironmental issues from the political and sociocultural issues. The focus of this chapter is to clarify the sorts of questions you should ask and answer as well as where you might turn for the information necessary to answer the questions.

So, why should you conduct a PEST assessment? Not everything of importance to industry firms is competition based. It could be, rather, the actions that legislatures or courts take, or the direction the economy takes, that can most broadly affect success. The recent (2008–2010) recession's effect on industry is well known—but if you are planning, don't you want to anticipate the timing and extent of recovery? Consumer beliefs and technological change may be harder to define or measure but can be even more disruptive. Consider how the spread of broadband Internet across the United States has threatened, if not destroyed, the old customer solutions for the music, home video, and electronic games industries. Easy downloading means that customers don't actually need the actual shrink-wrapped CD or movie—and this means that the old value chain of brick and mortar stores and associated inventory is no longer required. At a more fundamental level, even controlling the intellectual content turns out to be more difficult than in the past (hence the vigilance of the music and film industries regarding peer-to-peer file sharing applications like Napster). Identifying and analyzing technological shifts can help prepare firms to adapt (though, to be fair, the changes may come faster than companies can adapt, even if managers see them coming).[1] The reason you should undertake a PEST assessment is because it highlights the pressures and opportunities all firms in your industry will likely face.

The PEST Model

What is going to happen in the future, and how will it affect us? While we all take a shot at predictions, it turns out that some changes are of more interest or significance than others because they reflect long-term evolutions in belief or need or expectancy. Unlike fads or fashion, these trends can have long-lasting—even revolutionary—effects.

Ronald Inglehart, for example, has long been associated with a research project called the World Values Survey and describes several key trends in countries around the globe.[2] For example, he finds rising social support for environmental protection (think global warming agreements or green initiatives), for the expansion of women's rights (in particular, think of the striking images from Iran in this last election), and for increased participation in political-economic decision making in countries or societies where economies have been reasonably secure for a generation or more. He contrasts this "secular-rational" perspective with a "traditional" orientation that values respect for authority, nationalist pride, and the domination of business and politics by males and associates each with a particular stage in economic development. When economic security is tenuous and survival is the top concern, cultural values that emphasize stability and predictability (i.e., traditional values) are favored. Conversely, when survival is taken for granted (a postmaterialist perspective), people seem to value quality of life, personal happiness, and increased tolerance for other views. These are large trends, sometimes taking several generations to work their way through a society. As we'll see later, these shifts in values can manifest in all sorts of political or economic (or S or T) ways that affect particular industries.

There are a number of think tanks and specialists who view themselves as "futurists," or trendspotters, such as Alvin Toffler (author of *Futureshock* and *The Third Wave*), John Naisbitt (author of *Megatrends*), marketing guru Faith Popcorn, as well as many others. These are worth at least reading a bit about because, if nothing else, they bring topics and ideas to the table. Sometimes the ideas might seem obvious, such as the move away from a petroleum-based energy economy or the trend in health care from focusing on cures to focusing on detection and intervention. Some are more intriguing such as Thomas Frey's observations about how nation-state-based political structures and systems are overstressed and collapsing. This will lead to problems with how governments handle health care, retirement, and social safety nets. Frey suggests that national systems will fail and be replaced by more global systems. He also has an interesting observation about the rise of *business colonies*, or industry-based, temporary, and mobile affiliations of talent located around the current hub of activity to set up and solve problems before moving on.[3]

There are many sources of information about trends that we can find, but how do we interpret this material? That is the purpose of a model like PEST: It helps us frame, ask, and answer important questions that identify and describe the trend or event and then determine how it will affect the focal industry. This is a key point: Note the two elements of the answer. It is essential to describe what is happening, but unless you go further and figure out what it all means, then the description is not useful. Don't just describe the effect to yourself—analyze it!

Table 3.1. Political Changes for the Automotive Industry

P-effects
• Changes in CAFE standards
• Phase out of tax rebates on hybrids
• New emission regulations

The *P* in PEST stands for changes coming from the political and legal arena. In a general sense, governments interact with business to deter or limit unfair competition, to protect consumers from certain business practices, or to protect society from certain business practices. The issue in this analysis is the extent to which national, state, or regional government changes, or is expected to change, its position toward the focal industry. We usually see this through new laws from legislatures or through new or changed regulations from government agencies. For example, in the near past, the United States Congress passed laws affecting the survival of firms in the financial and automotive industries, considered placing caps on executive pay, changed how real estate loans are appraised, and is in the process of setting new greenhouse gas emission policies and laws. Congress has also considered an overhaul of health care systems in the United States, which will likely have a tremendous effect on hospitals, physicians, insurance companies, pharmaceutical firms, and medical schools, among others. Regulatory and governmental agencies also play an important role; for example, the Federal Drug Administration (FDA) recalls food and drug products for safety concerns and has flagged some (such as the new warnings for Chantix and other smoking-cessation drugs) and suspended others (such as Vioxx and Celebrex). The Federal Reserve is considering increasing reserve requirements for banks, which constricts the ability to loan money. Changes in laws and regulations usually reflect larger social trends. Certainly, laws can be reversed or revoked, but in general they only emerge when conditions are right.

So, once you've found the relevant changes, you need to finish by analyzing what they mean. For example, Table 3.1 lists some recent developments for the automotive industry. President Obama has pressed for an increase in Corporate Average Fleet Economy (CAFE) standards (or an overall fleet MPG average) of 35 to 39 MPG. That is the description—but what does it mean? One thing, certainly, is a change in fleet makeup, such as a shift away from trucks and SUVs toward smaller vehicles. That is not a decision made lightly, as it will call for the expansion of some plants and the closure of others as well as significant new investment in tooling and capital equipment. Automakers will have to introduce smaller models incorporating new materials and technologies. This involves two threats; first, there is only about two years of development time available to have the three years investment and production time needed for new vehicles. This is a very short window. Second, these changes will likely prove expensive. Cars can improve MPG by using lighter materials like carbon fiber or magnesium or ultra-high-strength steel, but they cost more. This will affect buyer willingness to pay and may dampen demand. In short, automakers have little time to make some very costly and risky decisions.[4] Here is a simple thought exercise to reinforce this approach: What will the end of rebates for hybrid cars or new emission requirements mean to the industry?

Some analysts include legal developments as a natural part of the P assessment while others consider it separately. In either event, the issue is that the legal system is part of the overall political governance system. Courts interpret law and, in the U.S. context, confirm or overturn legislation and thereby establish precedent. Therefore, legal decisions have the same ultimate effect as changes in law or regulation. To illustrate, California and a number of other states are seeking to impose emission standards that are more restrictive than federal standards. The process could go forward only if California is granted a waiver from Environmental Protection Agency (EPA) standards, so the state sued the EPA to

Table 3.2. General Political/Legal Issues

• Current and contemplated legislation at the federal, state, and local levels
• U.S. Trade policy changes
• Trading partner policy changes
• Changes in regulatory body scope, mandates, and policies
• Changes in funding and grant flow
• Changes in tax law
• Influence of industry groups and NGOs
• War and regional conflict
• Federal and state court decisions

force the waiver. Auto industry firms joined forces to file federal lawsuits seeking to block the grant of waiver in California, but in late June 2009, the EPA did issue a waiver to California, thereby permitting the imposition of higher standards.[5] What effect will increased standards have on firms in the industry? Is this an important decision?

Finally, do keep in mind that the scope of your inquiry need not stop at the national level. Particularly as international institutions, such as the World Trade Organization, and regional trading groups and governments, such as the European Union, grow in influence, industry firms will have to be thoughtful about what is happening elsewhere. Among other effects, the international scope of many firms means that what might seem to be purely domestic issues, such as merger or acquisition between two industry firms in one country, have to pass regulatory muster wherever the two firms compete. Table 3.2 summarizes areas of investigation for Political and Legal issues.

E stands for changes and trends in the general economic environment. The key issues are how changes in income or employment or commodity prices affect consumer willingness to buy and how input prices for the industry product or service will be affected. Note that even business-to-business firms need to be conscious of consumer decisions because demand changes will ripple back upstream.

The data you are seeking are basically macroeconomic indicators dealing with employment, inflation, money supply, production, and so on. Fortunately, these indicators are generally easily available. For example, The Conference Board's Economic Indexes include leading, coincident, and lagging series of indicators that give a general sense of which way the economy is headed. Leading indicators include average weekly hours worked by manufacturing employees, new orders for consumer goods, new orders for capital goods, new building permits, the Standard and Poor stock index, money supply, and consumer expectations.[6] What we

Table 3.3. Economic Changes for the Automotive Industry

E-effects
• Changes in interest rates
• Changes in exchange rates
• Oil price volatility

are looking for here are any changes in the direction and the magnitude of the change. If the indicators are trending up, then the economy is likely to strengthen. Most industries might benefit from that—but not all!

You should also be aware of other economic indicators that may be more industry related. For example, you might track exchange rates with major trading partner nations or the price of petroleum or other energy inputs. Also, there are occasionally sudden, near catastrophic shifts in economies. The 2008–2009 financial crisis is an excellent example. Many observers were caught by surprise—remember how fast and how far the stock markets dropped—and the effect has been a sharp limitation in credit availability and subsequent consumption.

Again, it is not enough to simply define what the changes or indications are; you need to determine the implications for the focal industry. So, for the auto industry, we might be interested in interest rates. If they are rising, what will this mean for industry firms? Higher interest rates mean higher payments for consumers, so this is likely to reduce demand. On the other hand, firms can keep sales stable by reducing the price of cars (or by offering special interest rates and absorbing the financing costs themselves), but this would mean reduced profits. Higher interest rates might also mean more costly or deferred investment for auto firms and higher carrying costs for inventory. In short, higher interest rates are likely to have adverse, or negative, effects on the firms. What would be the effect of a change in oil prices or in the exchange rate with, for example, Japan? Table 3.4 summarizes areas of investigation for Economic issues.

S stands for changes from the sociocultural arena and addresses both how the demographic structure of a society is changing and how values and beliefs are shifting.

Table 3.4. General Economic Issues

• Inflation rates, domestic and with trading partners
• Interest rate direction forecasts
• Monetary policy changes, domestic and abroad
• Changes in interest rate regimes by trading partners
• Industry revenue cycles and seasonality
• Employment rates
• Commodity price changes
• Industry specific/industry critical input price changes

Demographics are statistics about how a population is structured. We would be interested in changes such as population growth (or decline), the size of age cohorts or groups, education, ethnic background, income distribution, and geographic distribution. This is important data because it should indicate likely changes in consumption patterns and opportunities or threats (though some changes will be longer term than others). For example, Figure 3.1 illustrates the change in population by age group in 2010 versus 2000.[7] Note the bump for baby boomers (especially in the 45- to 75-year-old range) and the drop in Generation X populations. What are the implications for health care firms? One possibility is vastly increased revenues given the huge jump from the prior decade. This could also have a ripple effect on health care facility construction (or, conversely, on how health care is delivered), hiring, and education. According to the U.S. Bureau of Labor Statistics, two of the top three fastest growing occupations for 2008–2009 are home and personal health care aides.[8] For real estate firms, the news may not be good as baby boomers decide to sell out, which may lead to an oversupply of housing and subsequent erosion of real estate values. Note that this is just one way of describing population groups; there are other useful approaches.

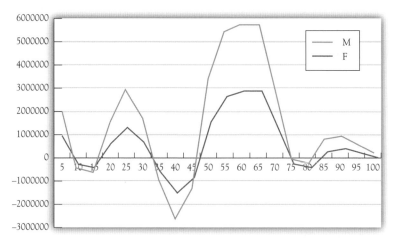

Figure 3.1. Population changes by sex and five-year age group: 2010 vs. 2000.

Table 3.5. Sociocultural Changes for the Automotive Industry

S-effects
• Age or income shifts
• Green consumerism

Other demographic indicators have similar implications for predicting changes in revenue or cost flows. Consider how the way a population relocates (e.g., from the Northern United States to Southern states, such as Florida, North Carolina, Texas, etc.) affects industries competing in both areas. Demand for everything falls in one and booms in the other. For example, construction would naturally increase in the destination states (new homes, institutions, businesses, and infrastructure) and so would sales of construction equipment, materiel (direct effects) as well as the need for labor. Or, for the auto industry, consider how changes in ethnic mix might affect advertising or product mix.

Value shifts are more difficult to identify and track, though we can find some useful sources. One of the keys here is to understand that collective social values change slowly and a timeframe of generations is not out of the ordinary. For example, the Civil Rights Act of 1964 prohibited discrimination based on race, but it took 45 years for an African-American to be elected President. In other words, it has taken a generation for general social attitudes to change sufficiently for this to happen. If Inglehart is right, values change as a function of the duration and depth of political and economic changes, but other factors appear to complement those larger change drivers. For example, the Pew Research Center's survey of Generation Next (young adults 18–25) argues that both technology and dramatic events affect values for this group.[9] Table 3.6 shows some of the key findings from the Pew Center survey.

Table 3.6. Generation Next

Generation next is . . .
• More politically engaged than prior generations and more likely to be Democrat
• More comfortable with globalization and new ways of working
• More likely to support immigration, gay marriage
• Very likely to value wealth and fame as life goals

What do shifting values mean to industries? If consumers actually enact values through purchases, then demand conditions will change. The change in environmental values over the past two generations has made green, or clean, solutions for firms in energy, transportation, and like industries increasingly attractive. In another example, Americans seem to have changed perspectives on the acceptability of alcohol consumption (based on health and social welfare concerns). One effect has been a flattened sales curve in the beer industry for well over a decade, but perhaps in the interest of drinking less—but better—beer, it has also meant an increase in the sales of craft beers. On the other hand, not all changes are really fundamental value shifts. A clear illustration comes from the first gas crisis of the 1970s when skyrocketing fuel prices turned consumers away from large and relatively inefficient American cars toward Japanese imports. Until the 1980s (after another, smaller crisis), it appeared that car purchases reflected a values change with regard to dependence on foreign oil or to environmental sensitivity. Cars were smaller and people drove less[10] (and Japanese-based car manufacturers grew significantly). Still, the return of cheap gas changed that. Once fuel prices fell in the 1990s, American buyers returned to large, relatively fuel inefficient vehicles, like SUVs.[11] Thus, what some analysts interpreted as changes in values turned out to be more influenced by economics.

On the other hand, short-term social changes can be very interesting (and threatening), particularly if your industry is engaged in short life cycle products. Fashion changes and the choices of role models can be remarkably influential. Every era has its dominant styles and consumption decisions, and the drivers are sometimes quite clear. For example, in the 1980s, the television show *Miami Vice* created new trends in how men dressed (you might remember the Armani jacket over a T-shirt) as did the Woody Allen movie *Annie Hall* for women's fashions in the 1970s. Fads, like the hot toy for Christmas or athletic shoes with roller skate wheels built in, are also relevant though difficult to anticipate. Table 3.7 summarizes areas of investigation for Sociocultural issues.

Finally, *T* captures how changes in technologies inside and outside the focal industry can affect choices. The key here is to go back to the idea that industry firms solve problems in a particular way.

Table 3.7. General Sociocultural Issues

• Demographic shifts in age, ethnic makeup, income, education, location
• Brand, company, industry image changes
• Consumer purchasing patterns
• Role model choices
• Media perspectives and reporting choices
• Advertising campaigns

Technological changes in the core of the industry's knowledge can affect how a problem is solved. Technological changes outside the industry can affect how the economic problem is even perceived—that is, this is not a problem anymore! Here is an example: Within the automotive industry, firms are working on alternative fuel and drive mechanisms. Hybrid (gas/electric) vehicles have been introduced but these are produced by the major industry players. New technological solutions, such as plug-in electric drives and new battery technology are permitting new players, such as Tesla, Bright Automotive, Fisker, and BYD Auto Co. (among others) to compete. New drive technology means massive investment for large players and a certain abandonment of current skills and competences, which turns out to be very hard to do! In other words how a problem is solved can change the set of firms that can compete.

Table 3.8. Technological Changes for the Automotive Industry

T-effects
• Lithium-air battery development
• Hydrogen fuel cells
• Petroleum substitutes

Table 3.9. General Technological Issues

• Maturity of industry and competing technologies
• Rate of technological development in focal and boundary industries
• Level of research funding (domestic and international)
• Technological licensing changes
• Patent regimes and lifecycles

Changes outside of the industry could also be very disruptive if they change how consumers perceive the problem. For instance, the Internet has changed the rules of who controls product information, pricing, and reputation for many industries. In the past, buyers were more constrained in the data they could gather because search costs were high. The web (and the proliferation of industry or product specific sites) has vastly increased the amount of information available and disintermediated industry firms. For example, car dealers were able to control pricing on new cars fairly easily because there were few ways for buyers to get really effective alternative pricing information. However, the Web and sites like Consumer Reports, Edmunds.com, and Car and Driver have vastly improved buyers' knowledge of car prices and financing deals, which has undermined the clout dealers had. Also, as previously observed, the technological changes represented by the spread of broadband technologies has disrupted, or is in the process of disrupting, industries that specialize in selling physical versions of electronic media, such as video and music or games and software.

Technological change can also lead to blurred industry boundaries; a process called *convergence*. Fifteen years ago, computer networking firms, like Cisco or Bay Networks, and telecoms, such as Nortel or AT&T/Lucent, served different customers or markets, but technological changes in hardware and communications standards (particularly the digitization of telephony) means they now compete in same industry seeking to provide end-to-end data solutions. Convergence is also occurring in the biotech/pharmaceutical industries, for cable television/telephony/data providers, and even in the early stages between computing and biology. When this happens, industries from both sides can be disrupted. An even more current example concerns how smart phones are beginning to rival desk top computers as the analytic and research tool of choice for many.[12]

As a caution, discerning the importance of technological changes is notoriously difficult, especially if you are assessing them at an early stage. A recent issue of *New Accountant* magazine listed some famous (though possibly apocryphal) comments by people we might consider experts. For example, a number of complete misses come from the computing/IT industry where IBM's Tom Watson, Jr. forecast a world market for five computers, and later, an engineer at IBM's Advance Computing Systems division wondered what benefit the microchip would bring.[13] Technological advances completely reconfigured not just the design of computers but also what was considered a computable problem, which gave rise to the popularity of, first, minicomputers and then personal computers. Still, given what the speakers knew at the time, the comments were not unreasonable. The point is be ready to be wrong (but be alert to factors that could change your judgment). Table 3.9 summarizes areas of investigation for Technological issues.

Summary

The premise of a PEST analysis is that disciplined questions, answers, and interpretation can uncover the significant trends in the general environment that will affect a focal industry and firm. PEST requires you to consider what is happening in the political, economic, sociocultural, and technological environments. Moreover, to be effective, it requires that you not just identify and describe these trends but that you also assess why or how they matter.

Some sources for PEST data are listed in Appendix 3.1.

Appendix 3.1

Sources for Industry and PEST Information

In the short term, these are useful sites for locating industry and PEST data:

- First, try a university library tutorial on locating industry information. Don't forget that most libraries also carry Standard and Poor, Dun and Bradstreet, and Moody's information in hard copy format. Finally, always be sure to identify and research industry associations (usually just an online search away) for current news on members, issues, and objectives.
- Also look for professional or technical associations within an industry—these are the practitioners of the art and science that drives the industry. Like industry associations, they often have newsletters or websites that highlight key issues of importance to the members.

- For a fast and broad approach to data, the LexisNexis Academic, Congressional, and Statistical databases are great. These get you fairly recent and high-quality information.
- Additional economic information sources include the following:
  - U.S. Department of Commerce Economic Reports
  - Commerce Bureau of Economic Analysis at http://www.bea.gov/
  - U.S. Department of Labor, Bureau of Labor Statistics at http://www.bls.gov/bls/proghome.htm
  - Federal Reserve at http://www.federalreserve.gov/econresdata/default.htm
  - The Conference Board at http://www.conference-board.org/ for information on economic indicators and consumer confidence
- Additional sociocultural (demographics and values) information sources include the following:
  - U.S. Census Bureau at http://www.census.gov/ipc/www/idb/index.php
  - Population Reference Bureau at http://www.prb.org/Datafinder/Geography/Summary.aspx?region=72&region_type=3
  - Pew Research Center: Social Trends at http://pewsocialtrends.org/
  - The World Values Survey at http://www.worldvaluessurvey.org/

In the longer term, I recommend the following:

- First, make sure you understand the overall value chain in your industry—what affects suppliers and buyers can affect you. In other words, you have to think about not only your immediate industry but the ones that surround you as well.
- Then, but *most importantly*, be an educated consumer of news about and around your industry. This means general business press consumption (and I like the *Economist* as an internationally flavored adjunct to *Business Week*, *Forbes*, or the *Wall Street Journal*) as well as reading in industry journals. In any event, read!
- Remember that you still have to judge relevance, importance, accuracy, and so on. Learn to be a balanced consumer of information. That is, not all commentary or material is equally valuable. Be discerning.

CHAPTER 4

Porter's Five Forces Model, Part 1

Barriers to Entry

Introduction

The economic theory about industry structure that you read in chapter 1 implies that profitability in an industry should go to zero in equilibrium (i.e., the accounting profits should equal the opportunity cost of the investment). However, we know that some industries appear to be exceptionally profitable while some are desperately troubled. For example, Table 4.1 lists the top five and bottom five industries in terms of profitability (return on sales [ROS], a profit margin calculation) from 2007 according to *Fortune* magazine.[1] Clearly, the industries differ pretty widely, but are these interesting results from the economic point of view? What explains the differences in outcomes? With a little work, we can estimate the expected return for the industries (i.e., the opportunity cost) and determine whether some industries experience above- or below-average returns.

Aswath Damodaran presents the following easy equation for this: *expected return = risk-free rate + (β) (risk premium)*.[2] For 2007, the risk-free rate was about 4.6% and the risk premium (average stock market return – risk-free rate = 5.5% – 4.6% = 0.9%). He also estimates industry betas (β) or volatility indices. His data indicates, for example, that the oil production, pharmaceutical, grocery, and semiconductor industries have betas of 1.30, 1.14, 0.78, and 2.11, respectively.[3] Given the previous equation, we should expect returns for these industries to range from

5.3% to 6.5%, yet the actual results are vastly different. Some industries (the top five) earn returns greatly in excess of the opportunity cost while others earn far below. Why? Michael Porter argues that industry-specific structural differences can generate these results.

Porter's Five Forces model is one of the best known and most used techniques for assessing the factors that most directly affect the profitability of an industry (see Fig. 4.1). Porter was heavily influenced by economists (particularly J. S. Bain and his protégé, E. S. Mason) working for the U.S. government in the 1940s, '50s, and '60s. These economists, while investigating industries that were believed to be generating unusual profitability, developed an approach that emphasized the relationship between structural characteristics of the industry and subsequent conduct and performance of the industry. Porter systematized this as five forces.[4]

The basic idea draws heavily on rejecting the key assumptions made earlier in the microeconomic discussion about industry structure. That is, if we were to relax those assumptions, such as free entry and exit, what would happen? Depending on the structural force, Porter showed how industry profits could be protected (as in the top five industries, perhaps) or drained away to benefit others outside the industry.

In this chapter, we'll focus on analyzing one of the forces: *barriers to entry*. We'll address the other four forces in chapter 5. The approach, as in using the PEST model, is to ask and answer particular questions and then analyze what the answers mean. At the end of this chapter, you'll be

Table 4.1. Comparative Industry Profitability

Rank	2007 Industry profitability ranking (top 5, bottom 5)	ROS
1	Network/communications equipment	28.8
2	Mining, crude-oil production	23.8
3	Pharmaceuticals	15.8
4	Medical products and equipment	15.2
5	Oil and gas equipment, services	13.7
48	Motor vehicles and parts	1.1
49	Food production	1.0
50	Semiconductors and other electronic components	0.6
51	Diversified financials	−0.9
52	Homebuilders	−9.5

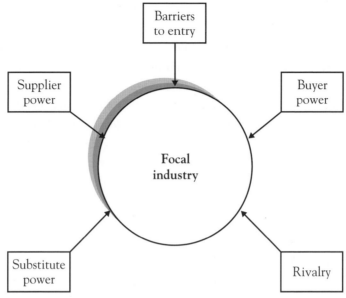

Figure 4.1. Porter's five forces.

able to describe the extent to which you expect potential entrants could dissipate industry profits.

Barriers to Entry

Barriers to entry are structural industry conditions that deter potential entrants because the cost of overcoming those conditions exceeds the profits the entrant anticipates. Recall how the presence of above-average profits—those greater than the opportunity costs—incites entrants because they want some of those profits. However, if the potential entrant concluded that entry costs are greater than profits, is it rational to enter? Such high costs keep rational potential entrants out and the industry incumbents continue to enjoy high returns. Our objective here is to understand whether this deterrence exists. There are many potential barriers to entry, but we'll analyze in detail a set that includes *economies of scale, differentiation, access to distribution, learning curves, switching costs, government policy,* and the *threat of retaliation.* However, in doing so, you'll develop, or model, an approach that can be extended to any other barrier. In assessing each barrier, we'll first establish what it is (a definition or standard; what it is we look for) and why it creates costs for entrants. Then, we'll focus on the key questions, such as, "Does the barrier exist in this industry and is it significant?" Finally, we'll examine how to analyze the results and draw appropriate conclusions.

There are a couple of key points to keep in mind as you go forward. First, this is a tool for analyzing an industry as a whole, not an individual firm. Second, establishing what firms are members of the industry is critical, and this is why industry definition (chapter 2) is so important. An overly broad or narrow definition can radically alter (and weaken) your findings.

Economies of scale (EOS) exist when the average cost of production decreases as output increases. It is useful to remember some basic accounting equations here:

$$AC = \frac{TC}{x} \, ,$$

where AC = average cost, TC = total cost, and x = units of output or production. We can break this down a bit further:

$$TC = VC(x) + FC,$$

where VC = variable cost (usually material and labor) and FC = fixed costs (usually capital equipment dedicated to production). Fixed costs (FCs) are those that must be incurred even if production drops to zero. Plug this into the first equation to get

$$AC = \frac{VC(x) + FC}{x} \, .$$

This is equivalent to

$$AC = \frac{VC(x)}{x} + \frac{FC}{x}$$

or

$$AC = VC + \frac{FC}{x} \, .$$

In other words, the variable cost component of average cost remains the same (as long as the technology doesn't change), but the FC/x element

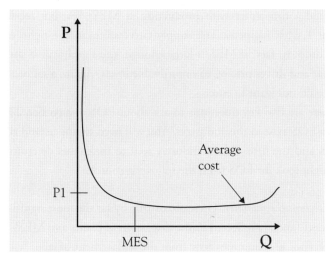

Figure 4.2. Economies of scale.

continues to shrink as output increases because that cost is spread over more units. The associated cost curve will look like Figure 4.2. Obviously, EOS are most often found in industries where production has been highly automated.

Another key point about Figure 4.2 is the point labeled MES. This stands for *minimum efficient scale*, or that production level where the cost curve essentially flattens out. Firms that produce at or beyond this level face about the same AC, but those firms that produce at a lower level face higher—sometimes much higher—average costs. MES is a function of where the product (or service) is produced, which is usually a plant.

EOS constitute a barrier to entry for several reasons. Let's assume for now that industry firms are price takers, which means that products are basically the same and buyers care most about price. This is captured by pricing at the P1 level in Figure 4.2. Note that if a potential entrant comes in with a production facility that is not at MES (some output to the left of MES), then the product cost may be too high. In fact, cost might exceed market price, which means losing money. If the cost penalty for entry under MES is high enough, the entrant faces losing all the potential profits through excessively high production costs. Therefore, a rational manager would not want to enter this industry if that were the only choice.

Could a firm enter with production at MES? Yes, but recall from chapter 1 what happens: The supply curve shifts to the right and the prices drop. In fact, if MES is large enough, the supply curve shifts out quite far and drives pricing to unprofitable levels. Again, a rational manager would not want to enter.

There are two key questions to ask about EOS as a barrier. The first is, "Do EOS exist in this industry?" You will need to understand the economics and the firms of the industry well to make this determination. You might look for EOS from the following sources:

- *Technical economies.* These are usually by far the most significant (and are reflected in the discussion of plants and MES). Technical economies arise from the replacement of labor with capital, so we should expect to see them in industries that are highly automated or capitalized.
- *Purchasing or commercial economies.* This is the benefit of bulk buying.
- *Financial economies.* Sometimes the sheer size of firms can give them clout in borrowing money at lower interest rates than those available to smaller firms. What would you need to know here?
- *Marketing economies.* These can be achieved by spreading the high cost of advertising on television and in national newspapers across a large level of output.
- *Managerial economies.* The administration of a large firm is improved by dividing management jobs and by employing specialists such as accountants, sales reps, and so on. Is this common or uncommon?

What you'll be looking for here are industry references, such as those in industry journals or trade association magazines, to topics such as

Key Qs

Economies of Scale

1. Do EOS exist and are they characteristic of the industry?
2. Are EOS significant with respect to supply?

purchasing terms or the scale of new plant construction. You might even find stories about single firms that appear to address EOS issues. These data can be cautiously extended to the entire industry if the firm is fairly typical in terms of size and configuration. (Although, note that anything characterized as unique to the firm or interesting is likely not extendable!)

If you do find evidence for EOS, the second question you must answer is, "Are they important?" What you want to accomplish here is an assessment of the potential problems with entry at scale and under scale. For the first, you are assessing the relationship between the MES for the EOS effect you've found and industry supply. The point is, if the MES is large as compared to current output (or if there appear to be oversupply problems in the industry), then an entrant is likely to find entry unprofitable. If the MES is small, though, entry is less likely to distort supply enough to cause profitability problems. Here are some examples.

In the brewing industry, MES has been estimated at around 5 million barrels per year at the plant level and as high as 21 million barrels per year at the firm level (The distinction between plant and firm MES is due to the fact that competition is national in scope though plants have a limited geographic service reach—hence, larger, multiplant firms). Overall annual national production in the industry is about 200 million barrels so a plant at MES represents about 2.5% of the supply. A firm trying to enter on a national scale at MES needs to add about 10% of existing supply. Both of these figures are large (especially since brewing industry growth has been flat to slightly declining for quite a few years).[5] Entry at scale will shift supply significantly and likely drive down prices and profitability, so EOS are a relatively high barrier to entry. In banking, MES has been calculated at about $2 billion in total assets. According to the Federal Reserve, assets for all U.S. commercial banks total in excess of 11 *trillion* dollars, so the $2 billion MES is far less than 1%.[6] Therefore, a new bank can enter without substantially shifting supply, and EOS are not a significant barrier. In long-haul trucking, MES has been estimated at around 500 million ton-miles, which is about one half of 1% of the overall market.[7] Shearer and his colleagues collated data from several industries and showed that the MES as a percentage of the U.S. market varied widely: The MES for refrigerator manufacturing was around 14% (this would be significant!), but the shoe production MES was only 0.2%, and cement was 1.7%.[8]

A caution, though: If production technologies change, what incumbents do from an EOS point of view might not matter. An example is the steel industry, where for decades steel was produced at highly automated integrated mills (like U.S. Steel or Bethlehem). These could begin with raw material of iron ore and coke and finish with rolled steel. The EOS here were enormous (several million tons of steel per plant), and for quite a while, they constituted a significant barrier to others wishing to enter the industry. However, in the 1970s, new technology emerged in electric furnaces that permitted the production of certain grades of steel at much smaller scales. Firms like Nucor or Chaparral Steel then entered with plants at one-tenth the scale of integrated firms.[9]

If the MES is high, an alternative for a potential entrant is to come in under scale. Clearly, given the shape of the curve in Figure 4.2, this means the entrant will produce at a higher cost—but how much? No two industry cost curves are alike, and the flatter the curve, the lower the cost penalty. As an example, in the brewing industry, unit capital costs for a plant at one half of the MES increase by 33%.[10] Similarly, in refrigerators, plants at two-thirds MES suffer a 6.5% cost penalty and in steel, plants suffer an 11% penalty.[11] These are pretty high cost increases, particularly if there is fairly standardized product pricing across the industry. Entering under scale in these industries can put entrants at a cost disadvantage, dissipating profits and making it less rational to enter.

Ultimately—and this is true of your assessment of all parts of this model—you will want to formalize a conclusion about your findings regarding EOS as a barrier. If you found that EOS do not exist in the industry, what would you conclude? If EOS did exist and the MES was a sizeable portion of demand, what would you conclude?

Differentiation is a popular word, and people use it in very distinct ways (from simply meaning different to a technical term from calculus). The word also has a very specific meaning in strategic analysis. For us,

Key Qs

Differentiation

1. Is there a willingness to pay more and brand loyalty?
2. Is this characteristic of the industry?

differentiation means that customers find extra value in a product or service and are both willing to pay more for it and are brand loyal. Note that for whatever reason when people care about a product or when they are loyal, consumers suspend their microeconomic assumptions that all products are the same and that firms are price takers.

For instance, some people are Coca-Cola drinkers, while others prefer Pepsi, and some have no preference at all. Are soft drinks an example of a differentiated product? Let's see how well this industry fits the definition. Are there different price levels or strata in this industry? Yes, in that Coke and Pepsi are premium priced products, generic soft drinks form the lowest price level, and in between there is a set of products that often fall between the two extremes in price (such as RC Cola, Orange Crush, Schweppes, and so on). Are soda drinkers brand loyal? We define loyalty as the willingness to purchase the same product or service when free to choose otherwise. In general, Coke and Pepsi (and many other competing products) are equally available for consumers (bearing in mind that restaurant chains often exclusively contract with one or the other major brand). If total market shares for differentiated products remain constant or even grow, then we can conclude that buyers are loyal. Is that the case here? The combined market shares of Coca-Cola and Pepsi increased from about 54% in 1966 to 74% in 2004 but slumped somewhat sharply since then to 60%.[12] Therefore, we can conclude that for most of the period, buyers were brand loyal, which makes these products differentiated. Still, if the data are correct about current trends, this is less the case now than it was just 5 years ago.

Differentiation can create a barrier in that entrants have to convince current product buyers to switch in order to gain business. However, if buyers are loyal, what motivation do they have to switch? In some way, entrants have to alter the value proposition for their product *and* both convince and inform customers about it. Our issue is really the second point. How would a new firm get this message across? Attracting new customers is substantially more costly than retaining them. A rule of thumb is a 5:1 ratio on costs of acquisition to retention, though in some industries, it can be much higher (e.g., 12:1 in the telecom industry).[13] Therefore, if entrants had to persuade loyal customers to switch through intensive advertising, samples, price cuts, and so on, then they would face incurring costs that incumbents do not. Therefore, potential profitability erodes and the likelihood of entry diminishes.

The two questions you need to assess for differentiation as a barrier are, first, is this industry characterized by differentiated products or services? Are customers loyal and willing to pay more? Based on the previous example, you know to seek evidence of price level differences or strata as well as some indicator of loyalty. Make sure that the higher prices reflect real choice and loyalty. If there is no real choice (limited competition as a cause, for example), people will pay more, but they will not like it. For example, in the air carrier industry, business travelers flying on short notice and in the middle of the week usually pay much more than passengers who have purchased tickets well in advance. The business travelers are not paying more out of loyalty but out of necessity because that flight is the one that gets them where they need to go and at the right time. Also, some consumers may be very willing to spend more but definitely not be loyal. Think about consumers of craft beers or wine who will willingly pay a price premium for a product. Are they loyal to a brand? Alan Newman, president of Magic Hat Brewing Company, has estimated that only about 10%–20% of the consumers of his beers drink Magic Hat 80% of the time. Rather, he characterizes these consumers as more loyal to a category of products.[14] Wine drinkers also do not exhibit significant loyalty to a specific winery. Rather, they tend to be consistent in their purchases of a particular style of wine (such as Chardonnay or Riesling) or a region (such as wines from California or Italy).[15] The second question is about the extent to which differentiation (if it exists) characterizes the industry. Here, imagine what an entrant would face in the soft drink market if, as loyal as Coke and Pepsi drinkers are, they comprised only 10% of the buyers? What would be the difference to an entrant if the loyal buyer share were 90%? In general, the more the market is made up of the loyal purchaser, the higher the barrier differentiation is going to be.

Again, draw a conclusion based on your findings about differentiation as a barrier. If you found that differentiation does not exist, what would you conclude? If it did exist and the share of loyal buyers were a small component, what would you conclude? What if the share of loyal buyers were high?

Access to distribution assesses the channels of distribution potential entrants have to use in order to provide their products or services to buyers. For instance, grocery stores are a distribution channel for food-stuff producers. In the brewing industry, beer distributors are the first part of the channel, then come retail outlets such as stores and taverns (though, to a limited degree, brewers can go directly to some retail outlets). In the auto industry, dealers are the distribution channel. The key issues for us are, first, describing the channel correctly and, second, determining if there are constraints, or bottlenecks—or the degree to which the channel is controlled by industry incumbents.

In the auto industry, for example, potential entrants need to find some way to put cars in front of prospective buyers. Historically, this has meant working with auto dealerships, as they are the immediate sales medium. What problems might a new auto manufacturer find in trying to line up dealers? First, most new car dealers have a flagship brand, such as GM or Ford or Toyota or Honda. They often have additional brands to complement the first but not always. Chances are a one-brand dealership will not take on other lines. Multibrand dealers might, but at what cost? Given space, capital, and personnel constraints, dealers that accept a new line will have to cut back on inventory (and sales opportunities) of existing brands. If the new brand didn't sell well, the dealer would be damaged—so how willing would they be to take on new, unproven lines?

Grocers face a similar problem. Shelf space is limited, and including a new product almost always means getting rid of some other product. This is a risk because the new brand may not sell. Some estimates are that 70% of new grocery product introductions fail,[16] representing an opportunity cost for the grocer. This is why they usually charge (often quite substantial) slotting fees, which can vary with the attractiveness of the shelf space.

Brewers, as mentioned, also have some channel issues. Federal law mandates that brewers work through distributors. Distributors are generally limited to a specific geographic area and, like car dealers, have a flagship

Key Qs

Access to Distribution

1. What are the channels? Do incumbents control or law/structure constrain access to the channels?
2. Are they costly to access?

brand or brewer. Anheuser-Busch's (A-B) distributors, for instance, often carry only A B products or those they are authorized by A B to carry.

You can see that gaining access to the channels of distribution may not always be easy or inexpensive. In general, the fewer channel outlets there are (because they are geographically bound or limited by law) or the more existing competitors control them, the more costly it is to gain access. Since accessing channels is a cost entrants bear, which incumbents do not, this erodes the potential profits of entry, constituting a barrier. Certainly, in some cases, entrants could attempt to create their own channels, but this would be very costly and certainly something incumbents do not have to do.

The key points to assess for access to distribution deal with understanding precisely how new entrants can place products or services before the buyer and identifying the control and constraints, if any. To the extent that incumbents do control the channels or law or structure (such as sparsity or geography) limit access, then the channels will require expenditures to access. For example, a new car manufacturer can implement large-scale advertising campaigns or underwrite extensive guarantee programs that could help sales, but these are costly and erode potential profits. Alternatively, a potential entrant can consider creating its own distribution system, but this too could be costly and time consuming. And as the costs increase, so too does access to distribution as a barrier. As always, draw a conclusion from your findings.

Learning curves (LCs) look like EOS—at least graphically—and create a similar cost disadvantage for prospective entrants, but the source of cost savings is completely different. In EOS, the source of cost differences lies in the way average cost diminishes as fixed costs are spread across higher output. The key issue in LCs is that the cost reduction comes from reduced labor (i.e., the benefit is in variable costs).

LCs were described first in the aeronautical industry as a way to explain why some frame manufacturers were consistently able to bid and build planes at lower costs than other manufacturers were. Inquiry found that workers who consistently did the same sorts of tasks got better (i.e., more efficient—that is, less time required, hence less labor cost). If you've ever put together a bicycle or other object complex enough to require instructions, you've probably seen that if you had to do it again, you could probably do it faster—which demonstrates an LC. Thus, firms that have experience will face lower cost structures than those that do not and this is not easily overcome. Figure 4.3 shows an average cost curve for an industry. Let's suppose that incumbents are already

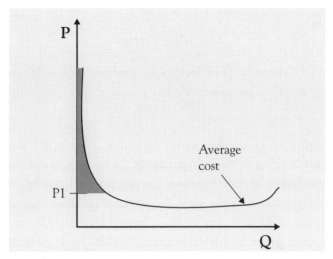

Figure 4.3. Learning curves.

operating along the flat, lower portion of the curve while entrants have to start at the top left portion of the curve. If prices were already established at P1, then new entrants would have to sell at that price. In other words, until entrants get enough experience to move down the cost curve, they sell at prices lower than their average costs. The gray shaded area of Figure 4.3 shows the losses entrants incur to get to efficient production levels—and if those losses are greater than the expected profits, firms are dissuaded from entry.

Technically speaking, LCs capture efficiency gains in terms of how much labor is required as output doubles. An 80% LC means that every time production is doubled, the labor required to produce output at the point is decreased by 20% (or is just 80% of what was previously required). Not all industries (or even many) exhibit significant LCs. What really matters here is the task or process. Processes that meet three criteria are likely to exhibit LC effects. First, the process must be *labor intensive*. That is, if you analyze the

$$TC = VC(x) + FC$$

equation, FC is usually low, and since $VC = (M+L)$, the L component (labor) has to be comparatively large.

Second, the process or task has to be *complex*. This is important because simple tasks do not permit or require much learning (that's why

Key Qs

Learning Curves

1. Do LCs exist? Are processes labor intensive, complex, and repetitive?
2. How deep or extensive is the LC?

they are simple). Lots of jobs have a high labor component but are too simple for learning to reduce significantly the time spent per iteration. Third, the process must be *repetitive*. The core process has to be done the same way every time. Thus, there are jobs that are labor intensive and complex but differ in greater or lesser degree every time they are done (construction might be a good example). If these three conditions are met, then it is likely the process exhibits significant LC effects.

It is probably apparent that LCs differ across industries. Some industries like aerospace or shipbuilding (or even locomotives) demonstrate LCs in the range of 80%–85% because the jobs are very complex and very labor intensive. Moreover, workers build the same model repeatedly. Other industries or processes (e.g., welding or electronics manufacturing) show LCs of 95%.[17] Some industries (especially bulk and continuous processing, where automation investment is high) show virtually no LC effects. Certainly, service industries show little to no LC effects, as each transaction is unique. Deep curves (like shipbuilding) mean there are significant cost advantages for incumbents. If the curve is 95%, then it is shallow and incumbents have less cost advantage. The deeper the curve, the more difficulty entrants have in overcoming the lost profits. Remember to draw a conclusion from your findings.

Switching costs are the sunk cost of investments customers have to abandon or absorb in order to switch to a new product. These are often expenditures for complementary goods or services to make a focal product work and are above and beyond the cost of the product itself. For example, if you owned a PC and decided to switch to a Mac-based machine, would you face particular transition costs to make the move? For example, would you also need new software? New peripheral devices? Don't forget that you would still have to convert data in old formats to new formats (or find and buy a bridge program that did it for you). Are training costs involved (even if not actual expenditures, then the cost

Key Qs

Switching Costs

1. Is the product or service complemented by difficult to reverse investments of money or time?
2. How extensive are these investments?

of time you might have spent learning how Word for Vista differs from Word for XP)? This might be aggravating for individuals, but imagine the cost to a firm in making a similar transaction. So, if sunk costs and complementary investments are high, switching costs tend to be high.

In fact, if the cost of switching is high enough, customers will not be motivated to make the move unless the new entrant can make it less costly. They can do this by providing training or installation, or coordination conversions, or any of a host of other ways, depending on the product or service. What these solutions have in common is that they all cost the entrant money that incumbents don't have to spend. This erodes the potential profits that accrue to entry, thereby making the industry less attractive. The key test for this, then, is to consider whether the focal industry product or service is complemented by other investments in hardware, software, learning, or other difficult to reverse investments of money or time. Note that the prior investment would have to be useless in the new context!

Restrictive government policy also affects the ability of firms to freely enter the market. This is clearly the case in regulated industries, such as the air carrier industry prior to 1978, public utilities, or even the restaurant and tavern industry in most states. To illustrate, if a person or a firm wants to open a business where alcohol is consumed, a liquor license is required, and getting one isn't just a matter of asking for it. In Pennsylvania, for example, the Liquor Control Board of Pennsylvania restricts the number of licenses available in a county to roughly 1 per 3,000 residents. If all available licenses in a county were issued, then potential entrants would be out of luck. This is not to say that one could not be transferred or purchased (there are a number of firms that could coordinate the transaction), but the cost is reportedly high, ranging from $5,000 to $400,000 depending on location.[18] Similarly,

Key Qs

Government Policy

1. Is access or entry to the industry regulated by government?
2. How extensive are the costs of entry compliance?

the City of New York limits the number of taxi medallions and auctions them off. As of 2009, the price to be a legal taxi operator in the city had risen to $766,000.[19] Thus, government policy can significantly affect the cost of entry.

Policy can also dampen competition through mechanisms like patents. In the pharmaceutical industry, for instance, as long as a drug is still under patent, no potential entrant can produce the identical compound. Similarly, government policy may preclude entry by foreign firms in key domestic industries altogether.

The key questions are, is this industry regulated by government? Are there restrictions on entry, and what is the cost of meeting or working around those restrictions (if possible)? Remember to draw a conclusion from your findings.

The final barrier we'll examine is the threat of retaliation from industry incumbents. Remember that new entrants reduce the profitability for all, so in some cases incumbents may be motivated to *threaten* to act to reduce the attractiveness of entry by reducing profitability prior to entry. There are, as we'll see, many ways to do this, but the key point is that if the potential entrant believes the threat, he or she perceives the industry to be less profitable even before entry and certainly even worse afterward. Therefore, the likelihood of entry is reduced.

Note carefully how this is worded: the incumbent does not actually do anything. (In fact, the incumbent really doesn't *want* to do anything.

Key Qs

Retaliation

1. Are industry conditions like growth, capacity, and so on characteristic of retaliation?
2. If so, to what extent?

Doing something really does hurt profitability!) Still, retaliation is a more credible or believable threat under certain conditions.

Potential entrants might more reasonably be concerned about retaliation if prior entrants have stimulated a strong response, if industry growth is slow, if there are high FCs, or if incumbents appear to have the resources required to sustain the response. We'll explore these conditions more when we discuss *rivalry* in the next chapter (for these conditions tend to lead to higher internal industry rivalry as well), but we can get a sense of the logic here by focusing on one element. Consider the FC problem. If FCs are high, then typically the incumbent firms want lots of volume to cover those costs and reduce average costs. New entrants push the supply curve to the right, creating excess capacity in the industry. This means that there is less volume per firm (all else being equal) so average cost increases, and since equilibrium prices drop with the new entrant, profits really dive.

How can incumbents threaten to retaliate? Mostly, they get the point across through public announcements and tactical actions. For example, in an industry where FCs are high, a firm might announce that it is proceeding with plans to add a new plant. (What would this do? Why is it a warning to potential entrants?) Tactically, firms might engage in price wars. Dropping prices without altering the cost structure of the industry automatically reduces profitability for entrants. The nice thing about price wars is they can (usually) be easily reversed once the threat diminishes.

The key issues here are to diagnose the condition of the industry and incumbents as described earlier. The more of these that apply, the more likely entrants believe they would face retaliatory actions, thereby increasing the barrier to entry.

What we've covered here is by no means an exhaustive list of barriers to entry. Barney[20] covers issues like proprietary technology, favorable access to raw materials or geographic locations, or plain know-how among incumbents. Porter also addresses capital requirements (the idea being that the more money is required to start up operations, the less likely potential entrants will attempt entry) and cost disadvantages independent of scale. These include control of proprietary technology, favorable locations, and government subsidies, among others.[21] An online search brings up yet more possible barriers. As you learn more about your industry, you may refine your list of barriers and include some that may

Table 4.2. Barriers Scorecard

Barriers to entry: Widget Industry	
1. EOS	1
2. Differentiation	0
3. Access to Distribution	1
4. LCs	−1
5. Switching Costs	0
6. Government	1
7. Retaliation	1
Total	3

be quite specific and exclude others. The key is to realize that you know which questions to ask: What does this barrier mean (i.e., what are the definitions or standards); why is it a barrier; does it exist in this industry; and if it does, to what extent is it a barrier?

Understand that just analyzing a barrier or reaching conclusions about a set of barriers is not enough. Ultimately, the idea here is to assess all the barriers (or those in your experience you think relevant) and reach a conclusion for the industry as a whole. When you analyze a barrier, you must reach a conclusion about whether it is strong or weak with respect to inhibiting entry. If a barrier is strong (or high), entry is more difficult and profits for entrants diminish. You should do the same for barriers as a class. This is, at least for now, not difficult. It is not crucial to be overly precise or worry about whether one barrier is stronger than another. We are interested in an overall view of the industry and still have four forces to go. Therefore, I recommend a simple (−1/0/1) scoring system for each force where −1 = *weak* and 1 = *strong*. If, for example, EOS exist in your industry and you deem them to be significant, score it a 1. When you do this for all barriers, you get a sort of composite and easy to understand score. In Table 4.2, I've analyzed an imaginary industry and found that four barriers are strong or high (or deter entry), one is low, and I am neutral on two. The highest score (exceedingly high barriers) is 7, the lowest score (easy entry) is −7, and 0 is neutral. How do you assess this industry? Is it easy to enter? Are profits being drained away to new entrants?

As a final observation, it is clear that if you are a manager for an industry incumbent, you want barriers to entry to be high to prevent others from competing profits away. It is a bit counterintuitive, but if you are managing a potential entrant, you also want high barriers. Under the assumption you can find a way to circumvent the barriers and enter, profitability will be enhanced because others are still barred.

Summary

In this chapter, you learned that certain industry structural characteristics act as barriers and can deter entrants and protect profitability. We covered seven such barriers. The key to applying a barriers analysis is to make sure you understand what the standard for each barrier is (i.e., what you are looking for), find the evidence for existence and relevance, and then draw an appropriate conclusion. No matter what you find here, though, recall this is just one (albeit the most complex) of the five forces. We'll cover the remaining four in the next chapter.

CHAPTER 5

Porter's Five Forces Model, Part 2

The Power of Suppliers, Buyers, Substitutes, and Rivalry

Introduction

In the last chapter, you saw that low barriers to entry can allow entrants to attack and siphon off industry profits, according to Porter. There are, however, four other significant forces that can do the same. In this chapter, we'll first assess how suppliers and buyers can extract profits from industry firms, as they have much in common. The first issue to keep in mind is that we are concerned with the *power of suppliers to and buyers from* the focal industry. Consider Figure 5.1; here we see that for the auto industry the suppliers include steel firms, electronics and integrated chip manufacturers, drive train and engine producers, and labor, among many others, while buyers include dealers, government agencies, and rental fleets. Focus on how each group applies power because you want to determine if each does or does not extract profits. You should not be concerned with how powerful the auto industry is *as* a supplier or as a buyer!

You will also learn how to analyze the ways in which substitutes for the product or service of the focal industry can erode profits for incumbents. Substitutes are other ways of solving the problem the firms in the focal industry solve; sometimes substitutes can be powerful enough to draw customers away. This can force industry firms to drop prices to retain customers—which cuts profits. Finally, you'll develop some tools for determining how rivalry among industry firms can compete away profits.

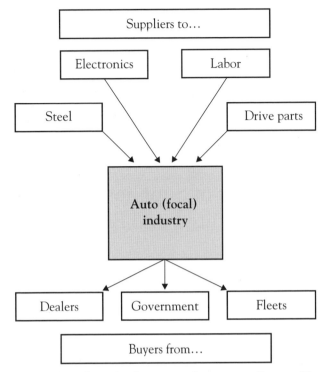

Figure 5.1. Value chain for the auto industry: suppliers and buyers.

It is important to remember that these four forces are not also barriers to entry as beginning analysts often assume. They are simply other ways in which profits can disappear.

Supplier Power

Suppliers are powerful if they can hike the prices of the goods or services sold to the focal industry firms. To the extent that the focal industry firms cannot pass price increases along, profits will be eroded (that is, the profits will flow to the suppliers). When we analyze supplier power, we need tests that show whether this happens.

To begin this, the first thing you need to do is identify the suppliers. The easiest way to do this is to make sure you understand the economics of the focal industry. What does it take to make the product

Key Qs

Supplier Power

1. Who are the suppliers?
2. Are suppliers more concentrated than the focal industry (FI)?
3. Are there substitutes for what they provide?
4. Are suppliers a threat to integrate forward?
5. Are focal industry firms significant to them?

or service? What are the tools, materials, assets, and so on that firms require to deliver the product to buyers? In other words, draw on the work you did in the definition of the industry to help you identify suppliers. Practically speaking, if you have access to the cost breakdown for the product or service, most of your identification problem is solved. Focus on the major industries as suppliers (e.g., those that contribute to 80% or thereabouts of the product or service cost). Further, make sure you focus on industries not firms; we are seeking a general statement about supplier power. For example, in the automotive industry, major suppliers include steel, drive trains, labor, and so on. In the air carrier industry, the major cost factors are airplanes, fuel, labor, and the airports themselves.

As noted earlier, suppliers are powerful when they can increase prices to the focal industry firms. There are four ways that this can happen, and these will be the standards or tests by which you assess supplier power.

Suppliers are powerful when they are *more concentrated* than the focal industry. That is, suppliers are comparatively concentrated when there are fewer firms in the supplier industry than in the focal industry or when the suppliers are dominated by one or a few firms. This leads to pricing power because there are few competing firms to which focal industry firms can turn. An extreme example is that of a monopoly or a single seller/supplier. Monopolists are well known for setting very high prices. If there are a few firms, we call it oligopolistic competition, and as long as these are fewer than focal industry firms, prices still tend to be high. The opposite condition is that of pure competition, where there are very many suppliers, each competing for focal industry firm business.

Table 5.1. Capacities of Major U.S. and Canadian Maltsters, 1997

North American maltsters	Share (%)
ConAgra	22.3
Cargill	15.2
Rahr	10.7
ADM	10.2
Froedert	9.5
Total	82.3

Table 5.2. Market Shares of U.S. Brewers, 2005

U.S. Brewers	Share (%)
Anheuser-Busch	49.5
Miller Brewing	18.7
Molson-Coors Co.	11.1
Pabst Brewing	3.4
Yuengling and Son	0.8
Boston Beer	0.7
City Brewery	0.5
Latrobe Brewing	0.5

We should develop some measure of how concentrated the supplier industries are versus how concentrated the focal industry is. In the brewing industry, as an example, key inputs include malt barley and hops as well as other agricultural inputs, packaging, and labor. Malting involves wetting the barley to encourage germination and then stopping the process by heating the grain. Major U.S. brewers, like Anheuser-Busch and Coors, all do some malting and therefore purchase barley for this purpose. There are generally many farmers growing malt barley. For major brewers, then, such suppliers have little power because the brewers are broadly indifferent to the type of barley, making the concentration of suppliers vis à vis the industry very low. On the other hand, since not even the largest brewers do all, or even most, of their own malting, they need to purchase from maltsters. Table 5.1 lists the output of these firms[1] as of 1997, and Table 5.2 recaps the data, presented in chapter 2, about the U.S. brewing industry as of 2005. I am willing to entertain a few years difference in data because getting exactly commensurate information is difficult and because the structure of the brewing industry did not change much from 1997 to 2005. Microbrewers may be a great deal more exposed because of specific recipe requirements, thereby reducing the number of suppliers that can meet their needs. Still, since major brewers account for about 90% of the market, what would you conclude about the power of agricultural input suppliers for the industry as a whole?

Appendix 5.1 illustrates two measures you can use to assess concentration. One is a simple concentration measure called the C4 (or the sum of shares of the top four firms in the respective industries) and the other is the Herfindahl measure. No matter which you use, you must do the analysis for both the supplier industries and the focal industry so as to draw a comparison. If your analysis shows that supplier industries are less concentrated than the focal industry, then supplier power, on this measure, is low. In this case, the C4 for the brewing industry is 0.827 while for the maltster industry it is 0.584. The Herfindahl scores are 0.293 and 0.095, respectively (the method for deriving the scores is elaborated in the appendix). You should conclude that the brewing industry is more concentrated than this supplier industry. Therefore, this supplier group is less powerful. Obviously, you may get mixed results where some industries are more concentrated and some are less so. What conclusion would you reach about concentration and supplier power then?

Another issue to consider is the locus of supply. For example, in the U.S. air carrier industry, carriers negotiate with airports for landing rights, gates, and so on. There are certainly thousands of airports in the United States, but if a carrier wants to add Denver to its route system, threatening to go to Detroit or Dallas isn't effective as a bargaining technique. In the scope of the Denver market, there is one good choice and a few less effective ones—but observe how the number of suppliers has diminished! If supply is a local issue, measure concentration at that level.

Another caveat, especially with labor, is to be thoughtful about the real negotiating unit. If workers have individual employment contracts, you can consider that labor as a supplier is diffused. However, labor unions, because they are a bargaining unit, represent a significant concentration for that supply input. Just think about how powerful unions have been in the past at extracting wage and benefit concessions from firms.

Suppliers are also more powerful when there are *no substitutes* for their products or services. The lack of substitutes reduces the ability of focal industry firms to shop around for alternate ways of solving their own key economic problem. As a historical example, industries in heavy manufacturing were often quite dependent on labor as a vital input. As previously mentioned, labor unions came to exert considerable power because of it. Increasingly, however, industry firms have invested in computer-based automation of all sorts of functions—from robotic welders and computer numerically controlled (CNC) machines to office automation. These devices are a substitute for physical labor, and as they become available and cost effective, they diminish the power of labor as a supplier.

In another example, steel is a significant component in auto manufacturing, but substitutes like plastic have emerged as body part materials. Some plastics may be more costly than steel now, but if steel suppliers hike the price of their product, plastics begin to look more attractive as an alternative. Put differently, substitutes put a cap on the price suppliers can ask. Labor cannot negotiate for wage increases as effectively (e.g., strikes) if the cost this would impose on focal industry firms is greater than that of a substitute for labor—because rational firm managers will quickly adopt the lower cost approach. If there are substitutes for what one group of suppliers provides, this weakens them. If there are no substitutes, suppliers are strong.

Suppliers are more powerful when they are a *credible threat to integrate forward* into the focal industry. Forward integration means that firms in one upstream supply industry enter the focal industry and become a new competitor. Referring again to Figure 5.1, we are interested in whether firms in the steel, electronics, drive train, or labor groups supplier industries can enter the auto manufacturing industry. Here is how the threat of forward integration works. Suppose focal industry firms can otherwise resist price increase demands from suppliers. This means that input costs are relatively low and profits high. Suppliers can threaten to enter the industry and, as another industry firm, share those high profits—which means that incumbents would become less profitable. So, suppliers can present focal industry firms with a choice: Pay us now, or pay us later.

What this depends on is the credibility or believability of the threat. There are two standards you might apply here. The first is based on the analysis you've done of the barriers to entry. The higher these barriers are the less believable a threat to enter becomes. The second standard is based on the economic problem of the focal industry and how closely the skills and resources of firms in the supplier industry match up with that task. As the task grows more complex, or the gap between task requirements and supplier knowledge and skills increases, threats to enter and do that task become less believable or credible. In the pharmaceutical industry, for example, biotech firms often play an important role as developers of new therapies that are then supplied to major pharmaceutical firms. Certainly pharmaceutical firms do a lot of drug development, but they have also developed assets in manufacturing drugs under strictly controlled processes subject to FDA oversight. They have also developed large sales forces of well-educated reps for the labor intensive process of face to face selling to physicians. Since most biotech firms are very small, technically oriented groups (i.e., mostly scientists and technicians with very small scale, developmental plants), would you consider a threat by a biotech firm to integrate forward into the pharmaceutical industry proper a credible threat? Why or why not?

Finally, suppliers are likely to be more powerful when the focal industry purchases are *not a significant portion if overall supplier revenues.* Porter argues that if supply industries serve a wide variety of industries and are not heavily exposed to any of them, then they will seek high prices from all.[2] However, if a supply industry is dependent on the focal industry for the bulk of revenues, supply firms will be wary of damaging the performance of focal industry firms because it would also damage them. The effect is to moderate the ability of suppliers to ask high prices. The standard you should apply here is a ratio of the share of supply industry revenues from the focal industry. The greater this ratio is, the less power suppliers are likely to have.

So, to assess supplier power, you need, first, to identify who the suppliers are. Base this on your understanding of the cost structure the focal industry faces, and make sure you are covering the inputs for at least 75% of the costs. Then, assess the suppliers in terms of the four criteria just described: concentration, substitution, forward integration, and share of supplier revenues. You can summarize your analysis by scoring each factor on the −1/0/1 scale described in chapter 4. If the test indicates higher supplier power, score that factor as a −1 and vice versa. Usually, you can expect that some factors will score high, some low, and some neutral.

When you sum the scores, you will have a final value ranging from −4 to 4 where −4 indicates very high supplier power and 4 very low. Draw on the whole of your analysis and reach a reasoned, comprehensive conclusion. Finally, note that these are not the only sources of supplier power but the ones we will emphasize here.

Buyer Power

Buyer power is assessed in very much the same way as supplier power. If suppliers exert power by raising the prices on inputs to the industry, how, then, would buyers exert power and extract profits from the industry? In general, buyers are powerful when they can depress the prices paid to firms in the focal industry, thereby capturing profits as some variant of consumer surplus.

Again, the first step is to identify the buyers or the entities in the next step of the value chain. Most of the time, buyers are the immediate downstream businesses that continue to add value. So, as Figure 5.1 shows, for the automotive industry, dealers and rental fleet firms are buyers. So too are governments, although they are more like final consumers than intermediaries. The point is individuals or consumers are not always, or even often, the buyer we assess here. As with suppliers, make sure you identify the key buying groups (i.e., account for at least 75%–80% of purchases from the focal industry). Make sure you understand the steps of your value chain!

As with supplier power, we will employ four tests to assess buyer power. These tests are concentration of the buyers versus the focal industry, degree to which focal industry products are undifferentiated, the ability of buyers to backward integrate, and the portion of buyer costs attributable to the focal industry.

Buyers are more powerful when they are *more concentrated* than the focal industry. The meaning and application of concentration is precisely the same as it was when illustrated in supplier power; although, a single buyer is called a monopsony rather than a monopoly. If buyers are more concentrated, focal industry firms have to compete for a limited pool of business. This tends to cause competition based on price (i.e., industry firms cut prices to win the business). The test or standard here is identical to that developed for supplier power. Again, appendix 5.1 should provide some guidance in developing concentration measures.

Buyers tend to be more powerful if focal industry products are *undifferentiated* or commoditized. Recall our definition of differentiation from the last chapter—the willingness of buyers to pay more for a product or service and be loyal. If products are undifferentiated, then there is clearly no willingness to pay more, and if loyalty is not an issue, what basis will buyers use to decide? This is one of the reasons that grocery stores generally have such low margins. Whether it is potatoes or hamburger or shampoo, the products being sold are generally the same from store to store. Certainly, grocery chains have been pushing two strategies to offset this: Either a bare bones shopping experience like at Aldi's or a more upscale experience such as Kroger Signature stores or Wegman's. But, particularly in the current economic conditions, buyers have not recognized very much differentiation and are increasingly price driven.[3] The standard here is to assess the degree to which buyers perceive and value differences among the goods or services offered by the focal industry firms. Why do buyers purchase what they do? To the extent that there are attributes in the product or service buyers value other than price, the less power they have to drive price down.

Buyers tend to be more powerful when they are a *credible threat to integrate backward* into the focal industry. Clearly, this means buyers threaten to move upstream in the value chain and enter the focal industry as competitors. The standards for evaluation here are the same as those for supplier power. You need to consider your analysis of barriers to entry because if the barriers are high, then the threat is less credible. Also assess

---

Key Qs

Buyer Power

1. Who are buyers?
2. Are buyers more concentrated than the focal industry?
3. Are focal industry products undifferentiated?
4. Are buyers a threat to integrate backward?
5. Are purchases from the focal industry a significant buyer cost component?

how well the skills and assets of the buyers match the processes of the focal industry. To the extent that they do not match, the threat is diminished and buyers are correspondingly weakened.

Finally, buyers tend to be more powerful *when purchases from the focal industry comprise a significant portion of their costs.* The logic here is not difficult to see: Consider your own shopping behavior when purchasing a car or home versus a magazine. The payoff to negotiating on high-price items promises to be very beneficial, so we tend to dedicate time to research and comparison shopping for big-ticket items. On the other hand, the gain from negotiating a lower price on incidentals versus the time we spend in the negotiation process is minimal. Therefore, the test for this criterion is to determine the portion of overall costs that purchases from the focal industry represent. For consumers, you may want to compare against annual income, while for businesses, you should have a more detailed breakdown of cost centers.

In summary, assess buyer power by identifying who the buyers are. Base this on your understanding of the revenue streams the focal industry faces and make sure you are accounting for 75%–80% of the revenue streams. Then, assess buyers in terms of the four criteria already described: concentration, differentiation, backward integration, and portion of buyer costs. Again, it is likely some criteria will indicate high buyer power and others low or neutral. Draw a comprehensive conclusion.

Substitute Power

Defining substitutes requires going back to the industry definition process. There, we found that the firms in an industry solve the interesting economic problem (i.e., meeting the customer need) in more or less the same way. That is, they all use the same general processes to produce, essentially, the same product or service. A substitute solves that same problem but in a different way. The substitute solution will meet the need (more or less, as we'll see) but with a different approach than the focal industry solution. For example, consider the aluminum canning industry, which is composed of firms producing two piece aluminum cans for food and beverages. You can undoubtedly identify some very popular substitutes for the aluminum can: plastic bottles or glass bottles or steel cans being three. How does the availability of such substitutes affect the price of aluminum cans? What happens if canners seek to raise prices to their customers? In general, strong substitutes siphon profits from the focal industry to those substitute industries.

Here are two important caveats for you. First, substitutes in this analysis are an industry level issue. If you are analyzing the auto industry, the substitutes for General Motors' products are not Ford or Honda because these are inside the industry. What are the substitutes? Public transportation, bicycles, or walking work very well as local alternatives in some settings, such as major cities, while air carriers are often very strong substitutes for long distance trips. Second, substitutes are rarely perfect, meeting the customer needs in exactly the same way and to the same degree that the industry solution does. This is why it is important to recall that customer needs are usually multidimensional. That is, a purchase satisfies a number of needs or utilities simultaneously. Substitution can be based on product/service quality specifications (will this do what I want or need), income (to what extent can I afford this), or time (is now better or can I defer). As Porter[4] points out, neckties and power saws are substitutes if you are in a hurry to buy a Father's Day gift. What you might perceive to be imperfect substitutes can work, though the less perfect they are, the less likely they will be able to meet needs effectively. In one of my graduate classes, for example, students debated in a rather hot fashion whether a salad is a substitute for a steak. What do you think? Go further: Is a book a substitute for a steak? The answer has to be yes, though the salad is a closer substitute than the book if consumers are hungry.

The standards for assessing the power of substitutes begin with defining the substitutes, which means you must envision other ways of solving the customer problem. Once these have been identified, assess them with respect to their price relative to the focal industry product or service and

Key Qs
Substitutes

1. What are they?
2. Do customers face switching costs from focal industry products?
3. How do the substitutes score on cost/quality tradeoffs?

their quality or how well they meet the utility requirements—how perfect they are.

Substitutes tend to have power when *customers have low switching costs.* This means that there are no sunk investments in material or learning to overcome. With no to low switching costs, customers can more freely purchase the substitute. Your test is to determine if there are switching costs for the product or service from the focal industry.

Substitutes also have power when they are less costly, of higher quality, or some combination thereof. Quality here again refers to the specifications customers have for the product. You can likely imagine the sort of internal discussion a customer might have in weighing these factors. For example, consider the choice between a trip to Europe and saving for college. What are the tradeoffs? What would you ask yourself?

Assessing the effect substitutes have on the focal industry is usually one of the most difficult of these processes, mostly because we underestimate the range of potential substitutes. Be creative here! Once you've identified good candidates, be thoughtful in analyzing the cost/quality characteristics. If switching costs are low and the substitutes are attractively priced or offer high quality or both, customer money should flow toward them and away from the focal industry. What happens if there are switching costs? Does this automatically end the analysis? No—be sure to carry through and research an overall conclusion. For example, in the auto industry, tooling for plastic body parts differs from tooling for steel parts so the latter are an unusable investment if a switch to plastic is made. However, as the price of steel rises relative to plastic, this switching cost becomes less and less important to the decision. As always, be sure to draw a conclusion consistent with the evidence.

Rivalry

The last of Porter's forces to be considered is that of rivalry, or the effect of competition among industry incumbents. In general, as rivalry increases, firms compete on the basis of price (i.e., by cutting prices), and falling-prices are not good for overall industry profitability. We will use five tests to assess the extent of industry rivalry.

Rivalry is likely to be high if *industry products or services are undifferentiated.* We covered this problem in the discussion of buyer power, but to reiterate, if products are undifferentiated, buyers have no reason to prefer one firm's products over another's except on a price basis. How then do industry firms win customers? By cutting prices—and this is true of industry firms in general. Prices and profits fall. Draw on earlier analyses (in barriers to entry or buyer power) to determine if products are undifferentiated.

Rivalry tends to be high when *industry growth is slow.* The rationale is that in slow growth environments, strategic moves by one firm to grow or gain share are felt more strongly by competitors than those occurring in fast growing environments. In the latter, all firms likely experience increasing revenues and may even be stressed to keep up with their own orders. In slow growing markets, gains by one firm are experienced as share and revenue declines by others, stimulating rivalrous response, which often includes price-cutting (hence profit-cutting) to retain share. The issue here is deciding what constitutes slow growth. There are several approaches you can use to decide. The first is to contrast industry growth rates with some larger measure such as Gross Domestic Product (GDP). Industry sector growth rates can also be a useful yardstick—for example, assessing transportation sector growth as part of the air carrier or automotive industry analyses—but the elements of the larger sector data may be tightly internally correlated. That is, because they serve similar purposes, there may be trends specific to the sector that could distort your assessment. GDP gives us a sense of how fast the economy as a whole is growing. By contrasting the national and industry trends, we understand whether the focal industry is high-, average-, or low-growth relative to all industries. Additionally, it may be useful to assess the direction of change. We can estimate how current industry growth rates, which are usually measured as revenue growth, compare to industry cumulative average growth rates (CAGR). An even simpler way is to compare recent annual growth rates. If current rates are greater than historical (i.e., the industry is experiencing a growth surge), rivalry is decreasing. If rates are lower, rivalry increases. Interpreting your findings requires some judgment. Growth rates for industries can vary widely, but if we use GDP as a center point, the issue is deciding what constitutes a great enough difference to be considered fast or slow growth. If GDP is growing at 3%, is a rate of 2% or 4% necessarily low or high? Or, are these near-average results, which indicates a neutral effect on rivalry? There is no simple answer, and it would depend more on the spread of returns for all industries. You can find information on long term and recent GDP performance from the U.S. Bureau of Economic Analysis[5] and, in a more global and comparative context, from the World Bank.[6]

Rivalry is likely to be high if *fixed costs in the industry are high.* Recall the cost equations from chapter 4 and the relationship between fixed costs, volume, and average cost. When fixed costs are high, firms need sales volume and the resulting production volume to absorb the fixed costs and keep the average cost in line. Therefore, you need to judge the extent to which industry firms face high fixed costs. This is not easy because there are few, if any, cross industry comparisons. However, if you recall that fixed costs are those the firms incur no matter the level of production and are usually related to investments in capital equipment, you can use industry descriptions to make the call. For example, if you've already determined that an industry exhibits economies of scale, you can reasonably conclude that fixed costs are higher than those industries that do not have economies of scale. Significant economies of scale can be a proxy for a measure of fixed costs. A valuable addition to this assessment is the information from sources like Hoover's "First Research Industry Profiles" These provide summaries on production and sales processes for hundreds of industries. For example, an assessment of the architect's offices industry indicates that economies of scale are low, that offices are often small, and that they are heavy users of computers.[7] Legal services are very much the same.[8] On the other hand, aircraft parts manufacturing is characterized by economies of scale and heavy investment in costly production equipment.[9] What would you conclude about the fixed cost structures of these industries? What do you conclude, then, about the scope of rivalry?

Key Qs

Rivalry

1. Do industry firms produce undifferentiated products?
2. Is the industry growth rate low?
3. Are Fixed costs high?
4. Are the industry firms equally sized?
5. Do industry firms face high strategic stakes?

Rivalry is also likely to be high when firms are more or less the *same size*. Appendix 5.1 compares two scenarios of industry structure where the top six firms have the same total market share of 90%. In one, each firm is the same size. In the other, one firm has 80% share and the rest have 2% share. Porter[10] argues that such asymmetries in size, as seen in the last example, reduce rivalry because a single firm controls the vast majority of the market and really doesn't regard the others as significant competitors. Thus, it is unlikely to respond much to rivalrous actions by the others because they simply can't do much. On the other hand, firms that are closer in size will be more directly competitive and engage in responses like price-cutting. One way to assess this test is to develop a Herfindahl Index score, which is a variation on concentration measures as discussed earlier and as described in appendix 5.1. If the score is low, rivalry will increase. If the score is high, rivalry is decreased.

Finally, rivalry is increased if firms have *high strategic stakes* in the focal industry. The issue here is the extent to which they are committed to that industry versus other business opportunities. To illustrate, if a firm is engaged in only the focal industry, its survival is directly related to what happens in that industry. Conversely, a firm that sees the focal industry as only one of several or many in which it participates (a diversified firm) will not perceive industry conditions and performance in the same way: What happens in the focal industry is less significant to the diversified firm's survival. Thus, the firms have different stakes in the industry. The issue is that with no other place to turn, firms with high stakes will fight desperately to survive while firms with other opportunities will be less willing to engage in low profit actions, choosing, rather, to exit and divert investment to where returns are higher. The test, then, is to determine the extent to which engagement in the focal industry comprises a key portion of overall firm revenues. The higher this is for industry firms in general, the higher rivalry is likely to be.

Table 5.3. Five Forces Scorecard

Five forces: Widget industry	
1. Barriers	3/7
2. Supplier	–3/4
3. Buyer	3/4
4. Subs	–1/1
5. Rivalry	–3/5

You can summarize your analysis of rivalry (as for all other forces) by scoring each factor on the –1/0/1 scale described in chapter 4. If the test indicates higher rivalry, score that factor as a –1 and vice versa. Usually, you can expect that some factors will score high, some low, and some neutral on rivalry. When you sum the scores, you will have a final value ranging from –5 to 5 where –5 indicates very high rivalry and 5 very low.

The last step of the industry analysis is to convert your force assessments to a common range for a summary judgment. In the last chapter, we ended with a simulated assessment of the widget industry. This is carried over in Table 5.1 where force scores are summarized. Now, for each, convert to the –1/0/1 metric. For example, barriers to entry score at 3/7. This certainly means that barriers are not low, but are they *moderate* (0) or *high* (1)? Generally, I would treat scores around the mean (i.e., from –3 to 3) as moderate and scores greater than 3 as high or strong. For four- and five-item tests, use a –2/2 range. When you do this, you weight each force equally.

We can summarize this chapter with a discussion of what constitutes an attractive industry. Each of the forces we have analyzed illustrates how profits may be diverted from firms in the focal industry. The tests that accompany each force compel us to dig in detail into what really happens in production, sales, and competition. From our results and conclusions, we build a picture of the industry as a whole. So, if you were a manager in the widget industry, what scores would you most like to see, and why? I interpret the following results from Table 5.1: Barriers to entry are moderate; supplier power is quite high; buyer power is weak; substitutes are powerful; and rivalry is high. In other words, the effects on profits for the industry would be neutral, bad, good, bad, and bad respectively. Overall, the widget industry seems to have a lot going against it, and we should expect profits to be low.

A final note: Twenty years after Porter developed his five forces model, he introduced new work on the relations between firms in an extended value chain.[11] The perspective in the five forces is that transactions are zero-sum: If suppliers win, for instance, focal industry firms lose. In contrast, Porter later developed the idea of *clusters* of firms in particular fields where interactions are much more collaborative and less competitive. He illustrates this idea through the California wine cluster, which is composed not just of vintners or winemakers but also of universities; grape stock growers; equipment manufacturers; firms that produce bottles, barrels, and corks; as well as restaurant and tourism firms. The perspective here is that the cluster is collectively interested in the final goal of delivering wine to wine drinkers. Porter argues that clusters foster better coordination and higher trust due to repeated interaction and physical proximity (most clusters are in a specific area, like wine in the Napa and Sonoma valleys of California) and also improve productivity and innovation. We've already seen how Porter anticipated this in the point about how suppliers who are dependent on a particular focal industry will be less likely to be aggressive in pricing. Here, we see it can extend to an entire (though localized) value chain. Clusters are not necessarily indicative of an entire industry, but we do have to note them when they occur—and they do occur quite often. In his 1998 paper, Porter identified roughly thirty locale/industry groups in the United States such as insurance in Hartford, Connecticut; farm equipment production in the Quad Cities area of Iowa, Wisconsin, and Illinois; or pharmaceuticals in the Philadelphia/Northern New Jersey area. This is not just a U.S. phenomenon; clusters are found around the world in virtually every industry. The important takeaway is that if such clusters exist, the competitive dynamics for firms within the clusters will differ from those outside the cluster with commensurate effects on profitability.

Summary

In this chapter, you learned how to assess Porter's other forces beyond barriers to entry. The systematic approach to doing this effectively is to first identify the relevant players in each force. Know which industries supply yours and which industries are buyers from yours. Then, apply the standard for assessment and draw a conclusion. Ultimately, you'll want to consolidate all the conclusions you reach into an overall assessment of the industry—and then run a sanity check against your expectations about the industry. If they are different, what does this tell you? In the end, the most valuable result from this sort of analysis is a much more deeply developed sense of the rules of the game, or a good feel for how firms are likely to compete, and a strong awareness of the opportunities for, and threats to, firms in your industry.

APPENDIX 5.1

Concentration Measures

1. C_4 or C_6 or C_x—a simple concentration measure.

$$C4 = \sum_{i=1}^{4} s_i$$

Where s_i = market share of the ith firm. The idea here is to sum the market shares of the four or six or x largest firms. The result will be somewhere between 0 and 1 with lower values implying less concentrated industries and higher values implying more concentrated industries. Using the data from the brewing and maltster industries in chapter 5, calculate the C4 ratios for both scenarios.

Table 5.4. Capacities of Major U.S. and Canadian Maltsters, 1997

North American maltsters	Share
ConAgra	22.3
Cargill	15.2
Rahr	10.7
ADM	10.2
Froedert	9.5
Total	*82.3*

Table 5.5. Market Shares of U.S. Brewers, 2005

U.S. Brewers	Share
Anheuser-Busch	49.5
Miller Brewing	18.7
Molson-Coors Co.	11.1
Pabst Brewing	3.4
Yuengling and Son	0.8
Boston Beer	0.7
City Brewery	0.5
Latrobe Brewing	0.5

Solution

- Brewing industry
  C4 = sum of four largest firm shares = 0.495 + 0.187 + 0.111 + 0.034 = **0.827**
- Maltster industry
  C4 = sum of four largest firm shares = 0.223 + 0.152 + 0.107 + 0.102 = **0.584**
- Note that the brewing industry is more concentrated because the top four firms control more share in their industry than is the case in the maltster industry.

2. **The Herfindahl index corrects for variation in market shares.**

$$H = \sum_{i=1}^{n} s_i^2$$

Where s_i = market share of the ith firm. The Herfindahl Index (HI) gives more weight to larger firms.
Using the same data, calculate the HI scores.

Solution

- Brewing industry
  H4 = $(0.495)^2 + (0.187)^2 + (0.111)^2 + (0.034)^2$
  = 0.245 + 0.035 + 0.012 + 0.001 = **0.293**
- Maltster industry
  H4 = $(0.223)^2 + (0.152)^2 + (0.107)^2 + (0.102)^2$
  = 0.050 + 0.023 + 0.011 + 0.010 = **0.095**
- Herfindahl scores are useful in comparing the structures of industries that are very different in terms of how evenly the market shares are divided. The brewing industry has much more share concentrated in the hands of a single firm than does the maltster industry. Thus, the concentration score captured in the H4 is almost 3:1 for the brewing industry. It is the same result as, but much more emphatic than, the concentration ratio scores.
- Concentration ratio scores are easier to calculate and are fine if the respective industry structures are roughly the same. The more they differ in terms of share distribution, the more an H score evaluation would be useful.

CHAPTER 6

Why Performance Differs

The Resource-Based View of the Firm

Introduction

The industry analysis we have just done gives us some powerful insights into what makes one industry so different from another in terms of competitive dynamics and overall profitability, but it doesn't do so well in explaining what interests us, as strategists, most. In all industries, no matter how attractive or dismal, there are firms that do much better than their peers and those (usually more) who lag. To illustrate, Figure 6.1 shows the performance of the major firms in the pharmaceutical industry in 2007, which was developed as part of *Fortune* magazine's annual Fortune 500.[1] Return on sales (ROS) is the simple gross profit measure. It is clear that there are significant differences in revenue, profit dollars, and margins among these firms. Which firms are the stars here, and which would be unhappy places to be a manager? What explains these differences among firms in the same industry? After all, industry conditions affect all industry firms in the same way, don't they?

It turns out industry firms indeed face the same conditions but respond differently to them based on firm specific characteristics. In fact, Richard Rumelt[2] has shown that across a broad array of industries and over time, business or firm-level effects accounted for about eight times as much variance as industry factors did in explaining differences in profitability. One key to understanding why firm factors matter more is to consider that Porter's model makes the simplifying assumption that all firms in an industry have access to the same technologies and resources (very much a restatement of the economic assumptions from chapter 1). What happens if this

Table 6.1. Pharmaceutical Industry Profitability, 2007

Firm	Rev	Profit	ROS (%)
Johnson and Johnson	53,324.00	11,053.00	20.7
Pfizer	52,415.00	19,337.00	36.9
GlaxoSmithKline	42,730.60	9,915.00	23.2
Novartis	37,020.00	7,175.00	19.4
Sanofi-Aventis	36,998.40	5,026.10	13.6
Roche Group	34,702.80	6,285.40	18.1
AstraZeneca	26,475.00	6,043.00	22.8
Merck	22,636.00	4,433.80	19.6
Abbott Laboratories	22,476.30	1,716.80	7.6
Wyeth	20,350.70	4,196.70	20.6
Bristol-Myers Squibb	17,914.00	1,585.00	8.8
Eli Lilly	15,691.00	2,662.70	17.0

assumption does not hold? What if firms can vary in their resource endowments or profiles? The purpose of this chapter is twofold: First, to understand what data, like those in Table 6.1, tells us about the performance and the competitive advantage of firms and second, to understand how resource heterogeneity or differences can explain performance differences. The analytic framework we will use for the latter task is Jay Barney's VRIN (Valuable, Rare, Inimitable, and Nonsubstitutable) model.

Competitive Advantage

We addressed competitive advantage earlier, in chapter 1, but to be very clear, we will want to separate two groups of questions about competitive advantage. The first is one of *existence*: Does a firm have a competitive advantage? How do we know? The second group of questions addresses *causes*: Why does this firm possess or lack a competitive advantage? How does it achieve above-average performance? So, if you want to determine *if* a firm has a competitive advantage, you are addressing the first question. If you want to understand what drives a particular performance outcome or *why* a firm performs the way it does, you are addressing the second groups of questions.

Deciding if a firm has a competitive advantage requires you to analyze profitability, but what kind? In chapter 1, competitive advantage was defined as abnormal profitability or profitability greater than industry average. From this, it is clear that you will need to two data points: a measure of firm profitability and another for industry average profitability. But what measure, and why? In Figure 6.1, we have two measures: profit ROS. Profit dollars are interesting (increases in, and the absolute magnitude of, profit dollars are the favorite of excitable press and political commentators) but not really useful. All they really tell us is which firms have the most or least of them. Such raw profits are often closely correlated with revenues so to simply focus on the number of profit dollars makes large firms appear better, which clearly isn't always true and offers us no insight about how efficient firms are at converting revenue dollars to profit. As was observed earlier, a better measure is profit margins (as a proxy for the ROIC). The simplest profit margin is gross profit margin (GPM), or ROS, which uses revenues and cost of goods sold (COGS) as a basis. It is calculated as

$$GPM = \frac{Sales - COGS}{Sales} .$$

Or, since *Sales–COGS* is just another way of describing gross profits:

$$GPM = \frac{Profits}{Sales} .$$

This is why the gross profit result is called ROS and is a better measure of profitability, as it corrects for size differences and tells us which firms are better at converting revenue or sales dollars into profit. ROS (or, alternatively, GPM) is a measure of efficiency. Related measures include *operating profit margins*, which deducts selling, general, and administrative expenses (SG&A) and other operating costs from profits, and *net profit margins*, which uses profits after additionally deducting interest, taxes, and so on. You can calculate these margins from company income statements. Usually, these margins will tell the same story about comparative efficiency but not always. For instance, Wal-Mart has often had lower gross profit margins than their competitors. Does this mean they are ineffective? The explanation lies in the fact that the discount retail industry does not have a cost structure like that of manufacturing where significant value is added to incoming raw materials. Discount retailers buy finished goods and then resell them. There is comparatively little labor or material input, so the COGS is fundamentally the purchase price from suppliers. Under these conditions, a lower gross profit margin could have two causes: Wal-Mart either is paying more for the same goods from suppliers than competitors or it is charging customers less for them. Which do you think is happening? A deeper look at this industry shows that Wal-Mart is particularly effective at the operational level (i.e., sales and general administrative expense and logistics), and it shows a much higher net profit margin than industry average.[3]

Profit margins tell us something about how a firm is doing but, in and of themselves, are not sufficient to establish competitive advantage. That requires comparison against other firms in the industry— the industry average performance. In Table 6.1, note the performance differences between firms in terms of profit margin. Which firm has a competitive advantage, and how do you know? How different should performance be in order to be considered indicative of a real advantage? On what basis should you construct an industry average performance metric? How long a period constitutes good evidence: Are one quarter's financial results sufficient?

With the information from Table 6.1, we can construct a first approach that develops a weighted average of profitability by dividing summed profits by summed revenues. This yields an overall industry average of 20.71%. This puts Johnson and Johnson right at industry average with GlaxoSmithKline, Novartis, AstraZeneca, Merck, and Wyeth right around that return, plus or minus. What stands out is Pfizer at 36.9% ROS versus Abbot Laboratories and Bristol-Myers Squibb, which are both at less than 10% ROS. From this list, at least for the year 2007, I conclude that there was one clear leader and a number of firms lagging behind industry averages. Other industries will vary. Note that while GlaxoSmithKline and AstraZeneca technically have returns above the average, they are not greatly above average. I recommend the notion of competitive advantage be reserved for firms that clearly outperform their peers, hence the focus on Pfizer.

There are several caveats to keep in mind here. First, this is a sample of convenience and may not reflect the pharmaceutical industry as a whole. This is why a careful construction of industry firms (from chapter 2) is so important. Second, the data cover just one year, and that can be deceptive as you may catch firms just after they have introduced a new product that will soon be imitated or after they have just written off investments that mark an otherwise stellar returns history. More data are better: Try to develop a sense of firm and industry performance over years.

Analyzing Firm Resources

Once we have established the presence or absence of competitive advantage, we want to understand why or how this occurs. What you are going to learn reflects a suspension of the assumptions made in chapter 1 about industry entry different from Porter's model. The base assumption for the microeconomic approach is that all entrants have access to the same technology and inputs as incumbents do. This is called resource mobility because resources should flow without impedance. In the late 1980s, though, researchers began to ask what happened if this assumption failed, if there were, in fact, mobility barriers that prevented imitation of profitable positions. If so, then firms that have carved out profitable positions with isolating mechanisms[4] should be able to enjoy above-average profits until competitors find some way to circumvent the isolation. This work and that of others, such as Birger Wernerfelt, Margaret Peteraf, and Barney, are the central ideas behind the resource-based view (RBV) of the firm. That is, what really matters is not the industry the firm is in but firm specific characteristics, particularly resource endowments, that define which firms succeed and which fail.

A resource is a factor of production (i.e., something that goes into the process of making, delivering, and servicing products or services). Thus, resources certainly include the materials used to make a product as well as the labor and the capital—but there are usually more interesting assets to consider. These could include specialized knowledge (such as that of scientists or engineers in R&D) or reputation effects (Disney is an excellent example here). Other interesting resources include especially efficient routines (firms that have implemented real total quality management programs could be an example or firms that are particularly effective at new product development and introduction) or socially based attributes such as organizational culture. Barney[5] categorizes this range of resources as physical capital resources (such as materials and machines), human capital resources or the knowledge and skills of individual workers and managers, and organizational capital resources. The latter are the outcome of group based work and include routines, planning and control or execution capabilities, and the relations between members of the firm and between the firm and its environment.

Another classification that may be useful is to distinguish between resources and capabilities (a learned or innate skill) or competences (what the firm does particularly well). That is, you might have a capability for playing the violin or growing organic vegetables or making specialized fly rods. That could be an important skill and requires certain sorts of more tangible resources (like violins and music or land or bamboo blanks, thread, and glue). Everyone can purchase the resources, but few can use them effectively. Capabilities are skills that use other resources. Sometimes, significant capabilities or competences can even be the result of combinations of other capabilities (i.e., higher level skills). For example, a "learning" organization's ability to recognize changes in environmental needs and effectively reconfigure or transform current capabilities to meet those needs could be a real competence (and advantage!).[6] Some guidance in assessing these more complex resources is discussed later.

Every firm has resources but it is resource heterogeneity, or the *differences* in resource endowment, that separates above-average firms from the rest. Obviously, not all resources matter in the sense of conveying a competitive advantage, so how can we determine the really important resources? Barney[7] has developed the VRIN model for managers and analysts so as to organize the critical questions for resource analysis. In this approach, resources are assessed to determine the extent to which they are valuable, rare, inimitable, and nonsubstitutable. If a resource passes all four tests, then it should be one that conveys sustainable, above-average returns to the firm, and that firm should demonstrate a competitive advantage. The discussion that follows develops the relevant ideas and tests for each step of the model. Note that this will be a time-consuming and extensive analysis because you must assess resources from a number of firms. This approach doesn't work completely if you restrict your work to your own firm!

The first step is to identify key resources for the firm in question. Firms usually have a vast array of resources available, so you have to cut the cognitive task down to size. Focus on the major value drivers both in the industry and at the firm level. What does it take to compete? How do firms do what they do? What makes them interesting? Select a set of key resources for the firm you are analyzing and take time to define what the resource is. For example, in the air carrier industry, every firm needs planes, route structures, gates at airports, and employees to do business. These are all resources that might be worth considering in an assessment of which resources, if any, contribute to a competitive advantage for a firm. The problem of definition requires that you really take the time to understand what the resource is and its salient characteristics. Southwest Airlines, like all carriers, has a fleet of planes, which is a resource. To stop the definition here, though, is to be too general. Southwest's fleet is made up of only Boeing 737s and this distinction will prove useful later.

Is the resource valuable? This is probably the most difficult question in the model to answer well. On one level, all resources should provide value, but since firms usually have a host of resources involved in production, this doesn't narrow the field. What we are interested in are resources that, as Barney puts it, allow firms to take advantage of opportunities or defuse threats. Another way of looking at it is to seek resources that *enhance revenues or reduce costs* in ways not usually covered in the industry rules of the game (i.e., based on your industry analysis). Here is an example: IBM dominated the early years of the personal computer (PC) industry in the late '80s and early '90s because of a particular resource. IBM was not the first to market with a PC nor, when it entered, was it the best known (that prize went to Apple Computer, which was very highly recognized). Still, it took little time for IBM to set the standard for PCs. The important resource here was IBM's reputation in the field. Computers were still very specialized and somewhat alien technologies for most buyers, both business and personal. The typical computer was

VRIN Model

V*aluable*. Does the resource create revenues or reduce costs for the firm?

  R*are*. Do few, if any, other firms possess the resources?

  I*mitable*. Can others economically create the same resource?

  N*onsubstitutable*. Can others economically create a different but equally effective resource?

still oriented toward the hobbyist who had a far above-average under-standing of (or tolerance for) programming at a deep level and was able to handle product assembly or modification. Because IBM had dominated the mainframe world for decades, though, its entry gave credibility to the PC as a legitimate business product. If IBM sold it, the complexity and unfamiliarity of PCs "didn't matter." IBM sold many PCs because buyers trusted the brand. IBM was able to gain most of the revenues and com-mand a higher price because of this.

Note that you need to be quite specific about how or why a resource is valuable. What makes Southwest's fleet valuable hinges on the fact that all the planes in the fleet are versions of the Boeing 737. This adds value not only because it allows Southwest to carry passengers (as planes do for every carrier) but also because the homogenous fleet structure reduces maintenance expenses, keeps crew sizes small, and reduces training expenses. Note how a general definition of the fleet (a set of planes, for example) would have led to overlooking these value sources.

In your analyses, then, you should be seeking to understand the par-ticular value contribution of the resource and how it is interesting or unusual. A hint might be the attributes the firm itself deems important, though this is not a completely reliable guide as managers are often myo-pic about this. A better idea is to understand how business is done gener-ally so that exceptions in revenue generation or cost management stand out. Always be certain that you can stipulate what the value is (e.g., the resource reputation creates additional revenues through volume and price or particular processes lead to exceptional productivity).

Is the resource rare? That is, do few, if any, other firms possess the same resource? If a resource is rare, it generates value in a way that other firms do not, which creates a competitive advantage. If you recall in chapter 1, Figure 1.4 shows how a single-firm industry looks with respect to profits. If a firm has resources that generate value in a way that others do not, then a condition of above-normal profitability exists. Determining rareness is a question for the state of the industry at the time of analysis. You shouldn't worry (yet!) about what could or will be done but just how things stand at the time of the analysis. A warning: Rare is not synonymous with unique. That is, a firm need not stand alone with its resource. This means there could be several firms generating abnormal returns. However, since you are interested in determining above-average performance and not best or top performance, this should not be an issue. There can be several firms performing above industry average. You will have to judge whether the number of firms that possess the same resource is so large that it is fairly characteristic of competition.

As a somewhat extreme example of what rareness means, consider the pharmaceutical industry. When drug firms in the United States develop prospective drug therapies, they have to comply with testing requirements imposed by the Food and Drug Administration (FDA) to demonstrate efficacy and safety. Because this process is very long (9 to 14 years on average), costly ($350–500 million), and usually unsuccessful (about 20% of drugs entering Phase I trials ultimately succeed), pharmaceutical firms are granted patents for the formulations.[8] With a drug patent, no other firm can offer the same formulation to the market. The notion of "same" is important: If even slightly different, the competing drug would have to go through the FDA process. Therefore, by definition, a drug therapy under patent is rare—at least, in the United States, since no other firm can sell that formulation until patent expiration. With some drugs, this protection, and the subsequent right to set very high market prices, can be the cornerstone of firm profitability. Drugs that are still covered by patents such as Lipitor ($12.9 billion in sales in 2005) or Plavix ($5.9 billion) are rightly called "blockbusters." On the other hand, when the patent expires, profits can drop 80%–90%, as there can be a number of producers of a completely identical product. Then, the only basis of competition is price.

Finally, consider how weakness in the resource definition can weaken the analysis. The simple definition of the Southwest fleet as just a set of planes would fail this test because all carriers have fleets. However, few carriers have a homogenous fleet and generate value the way Southwest does. One definition shuts the analysis down, and the other allows us to go forward in a useful way.

Is the resource imitable? That is, if the resource is now rare, can other firms develop the same resource? If others can imitate the resource, then they can stake a claim to some of the same profits or rents. If they cannot, then the focal firm has a chance to claim a sustained competitive advantage or one that persists over time.

There are two key ideas to consider here. The first is that imitation need not be exact; in fact, this is almost always impossible. For example, suppose your analysis of a firm indicates that the CEO is a real resource because she motivates well and gets tremendous buy in (hence productivity) from her staff. Can this CEO be imitated? Not in a literal sense, of course—but, is it feasible that other firms could find and hire equally motivational leaders? If so, then the resource can be imitated.

The second point is that imitation must be economically reasonable. Remember that the entire motivation for imitating resources is to claim some of the abnormal rents or profits that a competitive advantage firm is now getting. Now, to keep this very simple, suppose that if your firm can imitate that key resource, it will split the abnormal profitability with the firm that has the competitive advantage. Call the total above-average profits x and your share $\frac{1}{2}x$. How much are you willing to spend to claim those profits? Certainly, no more than $\frac{1}{2}x$, so there is a limit to how much potential imitators can spend as they pursue equality with competitive advantage firms. The expense cannot exceed the profits they expect to attain. If it does, rational managers would not pursue imitation and we have to call the resource inimitable.

For example, the Southwest Airline fleet turns out to be valuable and rare. This means it is helping to generate some above-normal profits. Can competitors imitate? Often, not economically because to do so would require radically changing route systems and operating philosophies. The large legacy carriers use a hub-and-spoke system, which requires high-capacity planes for hub to hub flights. To go to a 737 (a small jet) would make the hub-and-spoke system unworkable. Competitors could go to a larger jet style but these would have performance penalties on lightly used legs of the system (not to mention that smaller airports may not be able to handle large jets). So, in short, it is exceedingly difficult for existing competitors to create a resource that does what Southwest's fleet does. Though, note that entrants have no such problem. Jet Blue, among others, adopted the Southwest strategy at the outset, though it used a fleet of Airbus jets.

Barney develops three general explanations for why resources may be difficult to imitate. First is the problem of *path dependency*, or the fact that history matters. How firms develop or acquire key resources may be a function of the particular history of that organization. For example, Microsoft's involvement in developing the operating system for IBM's PCs was incredibly important, as it gave Microsoft control over what turned out to be the dominant operating system, and the key resource, in microcomputers. This has led to a two decade run as the dominant force in PC software. To put it differently, Microsoft was in the right place at the right time. Competitors seeking to imitate this key resource by introducing their own operating system cannot replicate Microsoft's path to industry dominance since the market has changed so much, and thus competitors now face some very costly problems with imitation, such as switching costs.

Similarly, Southwest Airline's tight-knit, cohesive organizational culture depends, in part, on the circumstances around the beginning of the firm. The preemptive steps taken by competitors, like Braniff and Continental, to keep Southwest from ever offering service created, among the founding personnel, an underdog mentality and a certain aggressiveness and willingness to work hard and pitch in to overcome the difficulties.[9] Developing a similar can-do culture is difficult because that attitude springs from history: To the extent the causes cannot be recreated, the outcomes will not emerge.

A second source of difficulty for imitators is *causal ambiguity*, or a lack of clarity about the link between a firm's resources and how they contribute to competitive advantage. If others don't understand how a firm gets the benefits it does, they cannot imitate. The performance may be the result of a number of small decisions or interactions specific to circumstances. To the extent that these cannot be easily observed, much less analyzed, the resource becomes difficult to imitate. This is actually so common that even firms with a high-performing, knowledge-based resource (like manufacturing know-how) often cannot understand how to transfer that same process to another facility and get similar results.[10]

The third source of difficulty in imitation is *social complexity*, or the fact that many higher level resources, such as reputation or trust, are the outcome of interactions between a number of people over time. Not only does history matter, we find, but so also do the people involved and their relationships with one another. The resource is experience based and experience takes time, which therefore makes imitation difficult. Suppose, for example, a firm's key resource is a reputation for trustworthiness. Is it necessarily impossible that a competitor could also develop such a reputation? No—but what would it take? Trust is the result of a myriad of interactions over time. To develop that reputation, a firm has to deal with its contacts (customers, suppliers, and other stakeholders) in a reliable, trustworthy way and not renege or default. Presumably, any firm can do this, but it will require perhaps years before that reputation is broadly accepted. As a side note: If reputation takes a long time to build, it takes very little time to damage, perhaps irrevocably. Consider the problems Toyota is having with respect to product quality, which has long been a calling card of that firm's high performance.

Another illustration of the difficulty social complexity presents is in organizational culture, which is often a critical resource for high performing firms. Culture is the set of beliefs, rules, routines, formal and informal hierarchies, and practices that emerge from the experiences of firm members over time. Culture sets the expectations for acceptable and unacceptable behavior by organization members. These expectations can be explicitly and formally spelled out in handbooks or contracts, but at an even more important level, they are often conveyed as newcomers learn about the firm through stories, legends, workarounds, and inside jokes told by veterans. Southwest has captured this in a relatively formal way by publishing for internal use a book that focuses on *What Positively Outrageous Service Looks Like at Southwest Airlines* and uses what are termed "legendary acts of service."[11] Real, deep-seated beliefs usually take some time to form and require reinforcement from others. So, if a firm wants to imitate the high performing culture of a competitor, what would it take? How could those valuable interactions among firm members be essentially replicated? Again, existing firms would have substantial difficulty in creating a similar culture because the rules, practices, and perspectives that workers have would have to change. Particularly to the extent that relations between management and labor have been rancorous (and the carrier industry has experienced many strikes and work stoppages over time), getting workers to change beliefs would be difficult. However, as in the example of Southwest's fleet, entrants might have an easier time creating a similar culture because they select members of a certain mindset and start with a fresh slate.

Another reason imitation may be difficult is because the high-performing firm has moved first or early and acquired or developed the resource at an extraordinarily low cost. This might happen because others do not yet recognize the value of the resource or because of luck. Resources that can be usefully claimed first include input resources but more often include assets related to space such as geographic location or shelf space.[12] As an illustration, Marks and Spencer, the venerable English department store, secured rights to central city properties through freeholds or long-term leases negotiated decades ago at very low per-square-foot rates.[13] Newer competitors cannot gain equivalent store space or exposure at near the cost. Thus, Marks and Spencer developed a cost advantage with the preempted real estate resource.

This raises a final concern about imitability. In a broad sense, potential imitators can suffer from *time compression diseconomies*, that is, there is just not enough time available to learn and emulate important skills or capabilities.[14] As we just saw, it may be possible for a firm to imitate the reputational assets of another, but it will take a long time because reputation is earned over time and through repeated interactions. You can't shortcut it. Additionally, even as imitators work to replicate the important resource, the high-performing firm can continue to build on the asset. An example is that of Wal-Mart, which pioneered so many supply chain innovations like hub-and-spoke distribution, electronic data interchange, and so on. Competitors could see how to replicate these processes, but even as they did, Wal-Mart kept raising the bar. For the period 1995–1999, competitors improved their efficiency 28%, but Wal-Mart improved by an additional 20% over an already much higher base. Thus, Wal-Mart was comparatively even more efficient afterward![15] If imitation takes much time, then the resource is often practically inimitable.

Still, even though there are reasons why imitation may be difficult, bear in mind that relatively few firms have real, long-term competitive advantages. Your job is to understand the attributes of the resource sufficiently to discern when real imitation is likely to be difficult (and for which firms, if that matters!).

Is the resource nonsubstitutable? This continues the industry analysis notion of substitution as a different way to solve the problem of interest. Even if imitation is not feasible, managers still have to be aware that other approaches may undermine the important resources that have provided a competitive advantage. If the substitute resource can solve the problem the customer has, then it becomes a legitimate claimant on the profits that previously went to the firm with the competitive advantage.

To continue a previous example, it may be the case that a strong CEO is not needed if the culture of the organization is strong. Thus, culture could be a substitute if it delivers the same productivity to the firm. In another example, Barney used Caterpillar versus Komatsu in the heavy construction equipment market.[16] Caterpillar had supply and parts depots around the world and, because of them, was able to repair broken-down graders and bulldozers very quickly. This gave Caterpillar a competitive advantage, and competitors were unable to cost effectively replicate the depot system. Komatsu, however, attacked at a different point: product quality. Can product quality be a substitute for the supply depot system?

Like the analysis of imitability, substitutes have to meet the economic reasonableness test. If it costs more to substitute for the critical resource, then rational managers will not do it. You should be able to demonstrate in your analysis why substitution, if it applies, is economically feasible.

Figure 6.1 summarizes the work for this chapter. Managers are interested in achieving a competitive advantage or above-average returns in profitability. This depends on the possession of resources that set one or a few firms apart from the others. The VRIN model shows us that if a resource is valuable but not rare, it can't be a source of difference. Therefore, at best it conveys parity or equality. If a resource is also rare, it provides at least a temporary competitive advantage since there are profits coming in that others don't get. It is temporary only if the resource can be imitated or

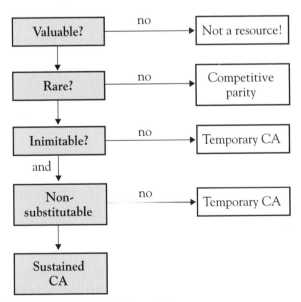

Figure 6.1: Applying the VRIN model.

substituted. If it cannot, then the firm has a resource that should provide a sustained competitive advantage or long-term returns above average.

This chapter closes with two pieces of advice. First, note that the high-level resources, also known as competences (what a firm does particularly well), should probably be investigated as composites of other, underlying resources. Southwest Airlines has a number of resources that likely pass the tests you've gone through but probably the most important resource for them has been the firm's competence at turning planes around at the gate and getting them back in the air. Historically, Southwest had been able to turn planes in 15 to 20 minutes versus an industry average of 45.[17] Fast turnaround means the costly resource of planes is better used, significantly reducing average costs. Turnaround time is not something that can be improved just through an effort of will, though. Southwest integrates resources like the fleet (small planes have small passenger loads for faster unloading and loading) and a point to point route structure frequently using small airports (which means no baggage transfers—just off and on loading). Southwest also pursues intentional minimization of amenities like food service (which saves time on restocking the plane), and a culture that encourages some rather unusual behavior (such as pilots helping to unload bags) together to drive its own fast turn time.[18] Imitating Southwest's turn time at the gate therefore requires that competitors be able to replicate a number of really difficult to copy resources—making this competence almost unapproachable, especially for incumbents.

Second, the real key to doing this sort of analysis well is being honest with yourself about your firm and your competitors. This may not be comfortable or popular, but glossing over competitor strengths or propping up convenient and reassuring internal assumptions about your own firm can be exceedingly dangerous. Andrew Campbell, Jo Whitehead, and Sydney Finkelstein argue that these misjudgments persist because of inappropriate self-interest (our biases color the way we perceive information), distorting attachments (such as loyalty to people or organizations), and misleading memories (similarities to what has happened to us before obscures important differences).[19] Since we are all subject to these influences most the time, it's difficult to know when you are really susceptible to distorted analysis. One recommendation that may help is to make sure you understand the real value proposition you are claiming for resources. A lighting firm I worked with, for example, prided itself on excellence in optical design and fixture manufacturing. In fact, the firm did produce very sophisticated and efficient lighting products, and managers were probably correct that it would take competitors years to catch up in terms of skill and catalog breadth. It was an article of faith in the company that such excellence mattered greatly.

However, what they missed was that many buyers didn't care about the extra 4% or 5% efficiency this firm's optical designs contributed to performance enough to warrant the price. Competitors who were able to use the same materials, were approximately as good in terms of performance, and delivered at a lower price suddenly grew strong. Thus, though optical design skills like this firm had were indeed rare and difficult to imitate, distorting attachments to the legend and culture of the firm led managers to overestimate their real value. Clear-eyed and objective analysis is absolutely essential to valid conclusions.

Summary

The performance of firms in an industry differs because of variances in their resource portfolios. Resources are factors of production, but the term is a broad one. Production isn't just the making of something but also the delivery of it at a certain price. Therefore, resources can also include reputation, knowledge, brand loyalty, routines, culture, and a host of other relatively intangible assets. These can turn out to be particularly important because they are often unusual or rare as well as difficult to understand from the outside. Under these conditions, firms with such resources can develop higher returns than others in the industry. That is, they have a competitive advantage.

To understand if your firm can achieve or defend a competitive advantage, you need to honestly and carefully assess the resources of your firm and those of your competitors. This is what Barney's VRIN model is intended to help you with. Note, though, the injunction about being honest with yourself: Don't underestimate your competitors and don't fall blindly in love with what you do well. It is better to anticipate and prepare for heightened competition because you have been clear-eyed than to be ambushed by events you dismissed.

CHAPTER 7

Deciding What to Do

Models for Strategy Formulation

Introduction

Chances are, most of you describe strategy as a plan—that is, what you are *going* to do. In the prior five chapters, you have developed methods that led you to thoroughly analyze what is happening in and around an industry. These conclusions or findings will help you build a basis for strategy selection. However, you can't do everything that might be possible, and

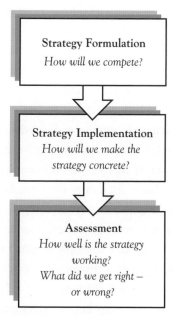

Figure 7.1. The strategy cycle (in part).

trying to do too much can be counterproductive. All firms have limited resources and capabilities, and some choices preclude others. That is, if you choose to do A, you cannot do B, and vice versa—so which is best? Why? Worse yet, it is often the case that managers make choices that conflict with decisions made at other times or by other managers in the firm. This means that parts of the firm work at cross-purposes, reducing efficiency and hampering competitiveness. The purpose of this chapter is to work through some models or approaches to consistency and coherence in your strategic choices.

Ultimately, strategy does involve planning in the sense that managers need to understand how the firm will compete and how, or if, it can achieve alignment with environment and industry. As we'll see later, the window for planning, and the specificity of decisions, can vary widely depending on the industry. However, in any event, it would be a mistake to regard strategy formulation as just a planning exercise. This doesn't capture the complexity or subtlety of strategy as a practical discipline. Effective strategy is not simply a planning exercise or a thing done once. Rather, it is a cycle of analysis, formulation, implementation, assessment, and adjustment. Strategy formulation, or planning, is one element of the process, and in fact, it may not even be a discrete part; it can be coevolving with the other elements.

Organizations need strategies for a variety of reasons other than mapping a future. A consistent and effectively communicated strategy can bind the members of the firm together by coordinating action. That is, a good strategy makes it possible for more organization members to act effectively without explicit guidance because they know what to do and why. Strategy also reduces uncertainty for managers. Finally, it can create, or at least should create, a lens or framework through which events in the industry or environment can be assessed. Managers don't just acknowledge these events but think about what they will mean to the firm. As Michael Treacy and Fred Wiersema note, the choice of how to compete "shapes every subsequent plan and decision a company makes, coloring the entire organization. . . . [and]. . . . defines what a company does and therefore what it is."[1]

In this chapter, we will first consider what a strategy should address in terms of scope. Thus, we will examine some well-known approaches to theories of strategic type from Porter, Miles and Snow, and Treacy and Wiersema.

Defining Strategy

The type of strategy we will discuss in this chapter is *business strategy*, or strategic business unit (SBU) strategy, which is distinct from *corporate strategy*. Business strategy focuses on a specific product and market, which means we can deploy all the analysis we've done to that end. Corporate strategy is about how to coordinate the activities of the diversified firm, which competes in multiple product markets and is beyond the scope of this book. A common approach to the form of a business level strategy includes the following three elements.[2]

First, establish the **scope** of the strategy. Who are the customers? Are you going to address all consumers or buyers or a subset of them? Is this demographically based or geographic? What do they value? This is, as we've seen in the discussion of how the industry firms solve customer problems and in the discussion of substitutes, a complex issue. Customer needs can have many dimensions and therefore many ways of solving them.

In addition, the scope of the strategy should also include how you solve the problem: The nature of the product or service the firm will provide. Define the value proposition of the product/service for customers.

Second, establish the **means**, or how the firm is to create and deliver the product or service. This is where managers can take advantage of the industry and resource analyses to intentionally carve out unique or at least rare positions because these are required for competitive advantage. As we'll see, this might call for the continued use of existing resources or the creation or acquisition of new ones to take advantage of opportunities. The strategy might also call for actions that shore up firm assets or positions that are under attack by others or subject to obsolescence. We'll cover a general way to think about alignment and types of investments in this chapter.

Third, establish objectives or ends. Strategy requires a goal that can be assessed. An old saying goes: If you don't know where you are going, any road will do—and this is true of businesses. Without a strategic goal, managers really don't know if they are doing right. The goals might be intermediate steps toward an overall desired position. So, for example, managers in an industry where scale and fixed costs are important might target a specific market share. A goal for another firm might be to be the most profitable firm in the industry. Think about

how these goals differ and what they would mean to the firm if communicated properly: How would share driven firms see sales opportunities differently than profit-centered firms? Should the differences
cause managers and sales reps to behave differently from one firm to
the other? Finally, the goals need to be time bound or have a fixed end
point. This doesn't mean that managers have to develop five- or ten-
year plans: Goals here might be relatively near term, depending on the
volatility of the industry.

When you've fleshed out and answered these questions, you will likely
have some statements and ideas that can be organized as a first pass at
defining what your strategy is. Figure 7.2 is a general schematic for how
that might look.

The goal is competitive advantage, so note how you need to identify
the resources (based on your analysis of the industry, your firm, and your
competitors) that would get you there. Do you own these resources or
do you need to acquire them? Strategy is thus that set of decisions that
gets you on your way to above-average performance. Implicit here is the
notion of means, or why to choose some resources rather than others.
This is the confusing, must–make-a-choice part, but there are general
ways of creating or formulating a strategy based on a consistent means
approach. We'll address three popular strategy typologies or classifications. According to their respective authors, strategic types can focus
thinking and efforts to attain certain ends and also warn us about other
approaches that may not be effective. In other words, these models can
guide strategic choice.

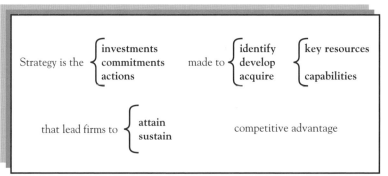

Figure 7.2. A definition of business level strategy.

Porter's Generic Strategies

Porter's generic strategies are well known enough that the concepts have entered general business language. According to his model[3] (see Figure 7.3), firms can pursue the strategy of being the low-cost producer in an industry, or alternatively, firms can pursue a strategy of producing products or services for which buyers are willing to pay a price premium called, as we've seen before, differentiation. Porter also acknowledges that both sorts can be pursued on a smaller (focused) scale. The useful idea from a "how do we create a strategy" point of view is that to pursue either sort of strategy, there are some actions or investment decisions that make sense, meaning they are consistent with the strategy, and some that do not.

Cost Leadership Strategies

In this approach, firms seek to be the low-cost producer in the industry (i.e., the means to competitive advantage). This should automatically make successful cost leaders above-average performers because at any given price

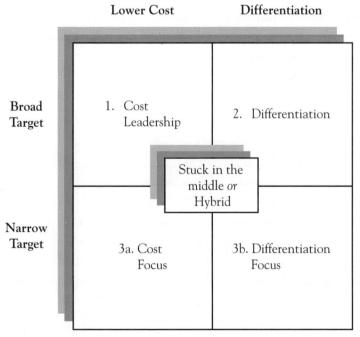

Figure 7.3. Porter's strategy typology.

level, the cost leader will have lower cost, hence higher profits and profit margins (see Figure 7.4). As Porter notes, though, that all firms, including cost leaders, have to produce products comparable to others in terms of product features and quality. In other words, there is a lower limit to features and benefits that buyers are willing to accept. Typically, there is one cost leader in an industry (though in some industries, a number of firms can be quite close in cost structure).

A cost leader's advantage derives from having the lowest cumulative cost in performing value activities compared to other firms across the industry. To clarify, Porter introduces the idea of the value chain, or sequence of steps performed, to transform inputs to outputs. Recall from chapter 5 (Figure 5.1) how the firms in an industry are part of a value chain extending from suppliers (and their suppliers) to buyers (and their buyers, as well). In that figure, the firms in the industry are treated as a black box, but in Figure 7.4 that box is opened. The sequence of steps illustrates how a firm generally adds value to the inputs it purchases and then sells to buyers. A firm may not perform all these steps—for example, sales and marketing or service may be outsourced—or may perform many more, as vertically integrated firms are wont to do. Nonetheless, the basic idea is that firms perform a set of activities in their businesses, and these steps have costs associated with them. In practice, the goal is to accurately describe the steps and the size, growth, and cost drivers associated with each activity—as well as develop an idea of how the competition does it. This is what activity based costing does.

Figure 7.4. An internal value chain.

Porter identifies a number of significant cost drivers (i.e., behaviors that affect how costly an activity is). These include the following:

- *Economies of scale.* Average costs decline as output increases. Porter observes that economies of scale can be found in almost all value activities but are not all equally significant. Note that diseconomies (i.e., increasing average costs) can also occur as activities grow large.
- *Learning.* This is more inclusive than strict learning curves (LCs) and includes harder to quantify experience. Thus, product design changes, production layout modifications, and even the resident experience from large but comparatively rare projects can yield learning cost savings.
- *Pattern of capacity utilization.* Activities with large fixed-cost components like plant and equipment will exhibit differing cost behaviors depending on capacity utilization or the extent to which the capital is used. For instance, in a cyclical production environment, a firm may choose a capacity to handle the greatest demand or a capacity to handle a lesser level and rely on inventory as a buffer.
- *Linkages.* These address relationships between parts of the value chain and how a higher level view can optimize costs. It may make sense, for example, to increase the costs of one step if it reduces the cost of another driver by an even larger amount. For example, paying more for higher quality inputs may reduce quality inspection and repair time. Similarly, to use the earlier example, holding inventory may be less costly than adding or maintaining production capacity for seasonal extremes. Linkages also refer to relationships with value activities outside the firm, such as with suppliers or buyers.
- *Timing.* First movers can capture or create important positions (like brand name and subsequent lower per-unit marketing costs) or learning effects. On the other hand, later movers can enter with new technologies or avoid legacy costs (such as labor contracts or pensions) or free-ride on the market developing moves of pioneers.

- *Discretionary policies.* These reflect what the managers of the firm actually decide to do on issues, such as product/service features and performance, service level, delivery time, warranty policy, human resource polices, and the like. Remember that firms must offer products/service that meet a minimum level of features and quality, so managers are not entirely free to choose—but, policy can make a difference in costs.

Firms can pursue a cost leadership strategy by changing the cost position of the firm so as to make total costs for the value-added steps performed comparatively lower than competitors. This requires control of cost drivers or developing a new value chain. To control the cost drivers, though, you have to understand how they actually work well enough to intervene. As Porter notes, it also important to understand how much each driver contributes to overall cost: The greatest benefit to intervention and control comes with the largest drivers. To illustrate, in the discount retail industry, Wal-Mart has implemented control mechanisms in several ways. The distribution center approach allowed the company to buy in larger amounts, gaining some purchasing economies. Wal-Mart was also a first mover in its rural stores, thereby shutting out competition and achieving lower per-store real estate costs. The company also learned greatly, from investments in IT, to manage personnel costs at sales and at inventory control and reordering.[4]

Firms can also modify or develop a new value chain. This probably requires even more analysis and insight than driver control does because it requires additional detailed understanding of how alternative structures would work. Chain reconfiguration can include deploying automation, new distribution channels, new production processes, and the like. Again, Wal-Mart provides an excellent example with the reconfiguration of supply and inventory. The usual practices in the discount retail industry were to order and ship on a store-by-store basis and hold the inventory at that store for eventual shelving. Wal-Mart developed a new chain wherein receiving and shipping are centralized at distribution centers, and stores are regionally served by deliveries. One result is that very little inventory is held at the store level (10% of store square footage versus 25% industry average). In addition, Wal-Mart's innovations in cross docking means that little inventory actually exists anywhere in the system. These changes to the typical value chain have provided significant savings to the company.

There are threats to a cost leadership strategy. These strategies are not intrinsically inimitable and competitors achieve similar cost position by deploying the same sorts of technologies or practices (if the gains to first movement are not great). Another problem arises when new production technologies emerge and the investments cost leaders have made are rendered obsolete, if only in certain markets. The emergence of minimills in the steel industry as cost-effective competitors to the larger, integrated mills was based on the development of the electric arc furnace, an innovation of the 1960s and 1970s. The new technology changed the cost competitiveness of incumbents dramatically and for the worse.[5] Cost leaders also run the risk of losing contact with the minimum features and the quality standards for the product, especially as consumer tastes evolve.

To summarize, firms can pursue cost leadership strategies by investing in the resources and capabilities that allow them to control cost drivers. These firms will be most interested in issues like capacity, scale, efficiency, productivity, the development side of R&D, and so on.

Differentiation Strategies

Firms pursuing this approach focus on attaining advantage through product or service attributes that buyers value enough to pay a price premium compared to other product/service offerings in the industry. The caveat here is that costs have to be around that of the competition. If that happens, differentiators can earn above-average returns because at any given cost level, differentiators have higher revenues, hence higher profits. There can be multiple successful differentiators in an industry because each can choose to emphasize a unique or particular bundle of attributes. Note well that *differentiation exists only in the mind of the buyer*. Firms can claim their products or services are differentiated, but if consumers don't see it that way, they won't be willing to pay the defining price premium. On the other hand, no matter how interesting or unique you consider a firm's approach to competition, if it is not charging (and getting!) a price premium, it is not successfully pursuing a differentiation strategy.

Buyers will perceive value when they determine that the product or service will reduce their costs or increase their satisfaction compared to competing products. In either case, the firm can capture part, but not all, of that value with a higher price. For example, firms can reduce buyer costs by offering lower financing costs (but remember, the firm offering this is absorbing a cost here) or make the product more efficient (think about the premium hybrid cars were getting when gas prices went up) or make the product more reliable. Firms can increase satisfaction by appealing to buyer needs for prestige or status (especially true in luxury items) by providing product customization such as bespoke or tailored clothing or emphasizing the quality of inputs, as Jim Koch does with the hops and barley malt that go into Sam Adams beers. Another approach is to focus on the reliability of outbound logistics as FedEx does or no-question product returns in customer service for firms like L.L.Bean or Orvis. Porter advocates analyzing the value chain to seek or create specific differentiation drivers. These can include the following:

- *Policy decisions.* Firms make choices about product or service features and how the product or service is delivered or communicated to the buyer. For example, the firm might position itself as a turnkey or full service provider (thereby absorbing some of the customer's set up costs), advertise more heavily than competitors, and so on.
- *Location.* Firms may dominate particular areas and thereby be more convenient. Wal-Mart, as observed earlier, pioneered stores in rural areas. Wal-Mart is very price competitive when in direct competition with K-Mart or Target, but when a Wal-Mart store is not near other stores, product prices are higher by roughly 7%.[6] Comparatively speaking, this still provides value to buyers as the higher prices are more than offset by the additional time and cost of driving to more competitive, suburban areas.
- *Timing.* Especially in brand or image issues, building that image early and reaching a customer set can pay off.
- *Linkages.* These, again, occur between stages of the value chain internally and between the firm and its upstream and downstream partners. From an internal perspective, product quality may be a cost issue for the producing firm as described earlier,

but it is also a perception issue for buyers, which is why, in the automotive industry, the J. D. Power *Initial Quality Study* matters so much. To the extent that the firm coordinates linkages to improve quality through control measures such as total quality management or through superior inputs and processes, then this is reflected in higher customer satisfaction with the product.

A firm can pursue a differentiation strategy through creating or defending rareness in how it performs value chain activities, or it can reconfigure the value chain in a useful way. Some examples of the first approach include:

Making the product fit the buyer's intended use criteria better. If the product is easier to use or if the firm provides training that helps buyers more easily master complex usage, this can justify a price premium. This is not a job for technical experts in the product—what is usually needed here is investment in personnel bridges between the technical knowledge and the user (who usually thinks rather differently from the expert).

Managing the buyer's perception through product signaling. Signals are indictors that lead people to draw conclusions about product or service attributes and value. These include the appearance, packaging, and placement of products; advertising and brand building; customer sets and influential users; and the like. The important thing here is how these characteristics guide the thinking of potential buyers, which means what these signals should be and how they are delivered ought to be central to a differentiation strategy. Advertising and marketing are investments in resources!

Identifying important new or unknown purchase criteria. Managers that can identify these have found a set of unmet or underserved needs, which can lead to effective new products. This requires substantial research work with customers.

Identifying and responding to channel and buyer developments. When buyers are changing (becoming more sophisticated, for example, or using new channels such as the Internet), firms can create differentiation by changing how those buyers are addressed. More sophisticated buyers may value sales techniques that better acknowledge or use buyer knowledge. In construction products industries, for instance, engineers are influential and respond to longer-term, relationship-based selling. Supporting such a sales force requires investments and measurements that are very different from "one-off" selling structures.

Firms can also pursue changes in the value chain to create differentiation. Thus, developing new channels (as Disney has historically done by developing theme parks to leverage characters) or integrating forward (as Apple has done by opening company stores) varies the traditional value chains in interesting and profitable ways.

Differentiation strategies can be threatened. Firms may charge too great a price premium for products or services. If the price exceeds the benefit to buyers, they won't buy. A common problem is that managers underestimate the need to signal value, arguing that the product/service qualities are self-evident. Relatedly, managers might convince themselves that product features are the same as benefits when buyers don't see it that way. Firms may also miss changes or evolution in buyer criteria. In the last chapter, the case of IBM as a leader in the personal computer business was used to illustrate how IBM's brand name created value in the new product market because it signaled competence and reliability when buyers were uncertain about the technology. Thus, when buyers began to figure out that PCs were based on Intel microchips and Microsoft operating systems, which were not proprietary to any one PC maker, and that any computer using these components was roughly equivalent, IBM's brand lost strength. The computer clone producers were able to thrive (and IBM fail) because buyers no longer derived sufficient value from IBM's knowledge of computers to offset the price.

To summarize, crafting a differentiation strategy will require identifying customers or customer sets (their purchasing and use criteria), devising products and service configurations that meet those criteria, and developing means of signaling those configuration characteristics to buyers. These firms will be more interested in issues like marketing and promotion, research (though development is also very important), and quality (or perceived quality).

Focus Strategies

In focus strategies, firms keep a very narrow or limited arena (target segments) of competition. This could be a geographically based segment or demographic. Firms can pursue either cost leadership or differentiation strategies here, and the criteria addressed earlier apply. There are two potential pitfalls. First is distinguishing between differentiation and *focused differentiation*. The latter is concerned not with general product attributes but with segments that have special needs. The example Porter uses to illustrate is IBM as a differentiator in the computer industry and Cray, Inc., as a focused differentiator. Perhaps an alternate might be Toyota as a differentiator serving multiple niches and Bugatti or Lamborghini as a focused differentiator. The second pitfall is failing to be certain that the focus niche is actually different from the general niche (as opposed to simply being part of it). This might be the problem for firms pursuing a geographic niche against firms that have national coverage. In order for this to work, the markets have to differ some.

Stuck in the middle is Porter's term for firms that are not disciplined enough to pursue one strategy and end up making investments in pursuit of two, usually uncoordinated, strategies. Porter broadly argues that firms cannot simultaneously be cost leaders and differentiators because the typical investments for one strategy conflict with investments for the other. Thus, firms that pursue both generally underperform because they are neither cost leaders nor successful differentiators. At any given price level, then, their costs are not the lowest, and simultaneously, at any given cost level their prices are not the highest. They are, in fact, getting squeezed in profits from both ends, which makes them perform worse than successful implementers of either strategy (see Figure 7.5). Still, per Porter, there are a few conditions under which firms can be both: if all other competitors are stuck in the middle, if the firm pioneers a significant innovation, or if cost is determined by market share and differentiation helps achieve greater share. Additionally, research in the automotive industry shows that Toyota and Honda have achieved cost leadership positions, and they still claim differentiated price premia in their product classes. That is, unlike other car manufacturers they were able to avoid a cost, quality tradeoff, and produce reliable, high-quality cars at low cost. This is attributed, in part, to the deployment of *lean production* techniques, such as just-in-time inventory, cellular manufacturing, and so on. Since these technologies are broadly available to manufacturers in all industries, hybrid strategies should be regarded as a potential (albeit difficult) option rather than simply characterized as stuck-in-the-middle.[7]

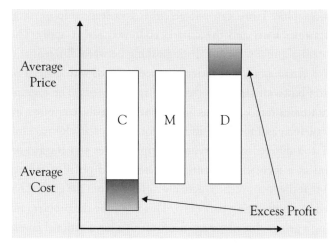

Figure 7.5. Generic strategy and source of profits for cost leaders (C), differentiators (D), and stuck-in-the-middle firms (M).

Miles and Snow's Typology

Another well-known strategy typology is that of Raymond Miles and Charles Snow.[8] From their perspective, strategy is about aligning the organization with the environment (i.e., given the opportunities and threats in the environment and industry, what resources do managers need to best fit in the industry). Strategy is also about sustaining such *coalignment* but because conditions keep changing, this is a moving target.

Miles and Snow argue that the process of sustained alignment with the environment requires that managers be sensitive to industry dynamics. That is, conditions change and organizations ought to change to reflect that. Their model of the *adaptive cycle* illustrates the decisions managers must continuously and simultaneously face and resolve.

The *entrepreneurial problem* is concerned with what to sell. In other words, managers addressing this are making a commitment to a particular product-market domain, or what is sold to whom, which is an answer to the definition of strategic scope. From an adaptation perspective, one of the serious challenges is that changes outside often affect the value of the entrepreneurial solution (see PEST from chapter 3, for example), which means that it must be revisited to realign products or services with needs. The volatility of the industry (that is, how fast changes in the problem buyers have or the solutions to it are developed) matters greatly.

The *engineering problem* deals with how to make or produce the entrepreneurial solution. These are the choices of production technologies, distribution, and production control and communication systems. This also bears revisiting because new technology production processes arise, as do challenges to efficiency of the current approach (e.g., volume increases might make investing in more automated production feasible while standing pat could be costly).

The *administrative problem* centers around how to systematize or routinize the successful activities developed in pursuit of the entrepreneurial and engineering problems. In other words, mangers want to avoid reinventing the wheel. At the same time, managers have to be cautious not to stifle creativity and innovation. Therefore, the administrative problem calls for choosing the right mix of systems and processes to best meet environmental demands.

Based on the adaptive cycle and the responses managers choose, Miles and Snow describe a range of strategies firms can employ. These are organizational types that occupy a spectrum from strategic D*efenders* to P*rospectors* (see Figure 7.6).

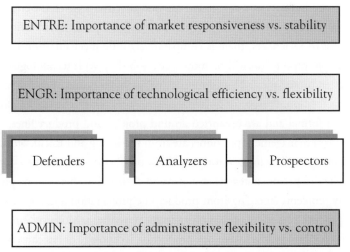

Figure 7.6. Miles and Snow's strategic typology and the adaptive cycle (darker is more important to a strategy).

Defenders are firms that desire a stable product or service market. Their solution to the entrepreneurial problem is usually a narrow offering in terms of who is served and with what. The focus of growth is deeper into the existing market, not into new markets. The Defender's solution to the engineering problem is to become exceedingly efficient technologically, usually leveraging a single core production technology. The administrative problem is one of control and efficiency where finance and production staffs tend to be the most powerful. The Defender organization is usually hierarchical where reporting structures matter and are built along functional lines, such as production or sales, and so on. The executive group tends to have risen through the company ranks and is therefore long tenured and planning driven. A key assumption for the strategist in the Defender mode is that the environment is fairly stable. The noteworthy strategic investments will usually be in production capital and processes.

A benefit to this approach is that if successful, Defenders are difficult to dislodge. The drawback is that industry shifts in customer needs or production technologies can be very disruptive.

Prospectors are, in general, the opposite of Defenders. The entrepreneurial challenge is to identify and exploit new market opportunities through new product or service introduction. For Prospectors, the product or service line should constantly be evolving and changing. The competitive environment is perceived as dynamic and a key role is monitoring (e.g., PEST and industry assessments) to respond effectively. Given the entrepreneurial issues, the engineering approach is to keep production flexible. In contrast to Defenders, there is comparatively little mechanization or routinization; production will be more like a job shop with technologies that are often prototypical. The administrative problem is one of coordination and facilitation. Prospector governance structures tend to be less hierarchical and formal and are organized around projects and product lines. The dominant management personnel are from marketing and R&D. Strategic investments will be in monitoring and fast product development.

The Prospector strategy is responsive to change, but there can be profitability problems emerging from product line proliferation and cost. Extensive product lines add significant management overhead. Moreover, since the firm is not heavily invested in one production technology or has chosen general rather than focused technologies so as to switch if need be, average costs can be adversely affected. Growth for Prospectors tends to be in spurts or irregular, which makes cash flow management more difficult. Internal coordination is likely to be tough, as there are many fairly autonomous agents.

Analyzers are very much a middle ground between Defenders and Prospectors and exhibit characteristics of both. Their entrepreneurial problem is to respond to new market opportunities *and* maintain the current loyal customer base. Growth is through line extensions and attacking new markets. They address the engineering problem with a "dual technological core" that seeks to balance high efficiency and high responsiveness. In other words, Analyzers have committed to more rationalized production than Prospectors but are not solely cost or efficiency focused in the way Defenders are. The administration problem is really structural: How can management control the dynamics of both approaches? In this strategy, marketing and production staffers share power and influence. The organizational structure tends to matrix management where managers have responsibilities in both product groups and functional roles.

Even though Analyzers emphasize stability and flexibility simultaneously, there is a limit to how far they can go in either direction, which means they can get outflanked by more specialized strategies on either cost or customer responsiveness as the industry or environment evolves. Trying to maintain two different philosophies of competition and control simultaneously is exceedingly difficult. Thus, Analyzers that lose balance tend to be both inefficient and ineffective.

Outside the range of strategies lie Reactors, or organizations that do not engage their environment consistently. Miles and Snow argue the Reactor approach is not a strategy per se but the outcome of not pursuing one of the three main types properly. For Reactors, a failure to articulate or communicate the strategy can lead to uncoordinated investments and choices. Since all three of the mainline strategies impose consistency in investment and how to respond to the market, Reactors are a contrast in how they might respond in all ways at one time or another. Reactors have been described as comparatively dysfunctional.

Treacy and Wiersema's Value Disciplines

In the 1990s, Treacy and Wiersema introduced their notion of value disciplines, or ways that firms can organize and execute to deliver specific value to a customer base.[9] The big idea here is the focus on what customers value—a continuation of the work done in PEST analysis that asks us to identify the drivers of choice for customers.

Treacy and Wiersema develop their classification scheme by contrasting a customer cost focus (that is, an overall cost position, which includes the purchase price plus maintenance, service, and convenience—or inconvenience—costs) with a benefits focus. Benefits are the attributes of the product or service that improve the performance or experience of the customer through product features, reputation, or service, such as advice or customization. From this, three goals emerge: Customers want the best price, the best product, or the best overall solution. Treacy and Wiersema argue that these goals can be met through the appropriate three value disciplines (or organizing structures), which are defined as operational excellence, product leadership, and customer intimacy (see Figure 7.7) These are distinct ways by which managers can focus their organizations and align efforts and

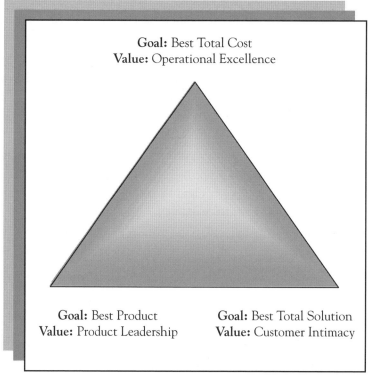

Goal: Best Total Cost
Value: Operational Excellence

Goal: Best Product
Value: Product Leadership

Goal: Best Total Solution
Value: Customer Intimacy

Figure 7.7. The value discipline spectrum.

Table 7.1. Treacy and Wiersema's Rules

Value discipline rules of competition
• Focus on excelling in *one* dimension of customer value *and*
• Achieve at least basic competence in the other two dimensions (can't drop below!)
• Improve year after year in the value discipline—stay ahead of imitators
• Organize the firm to deliver the value

investments. As they point out, firms cannot please all customers, so the choice of which set to target will have significant effects on what the firm looks like. Thus, they focus on how the driving ideas behind each discipline should be reflected in operating processes and focus, organizational structure, management systems, and culture.

Operational Excellence: Deriving the Best Total Cost

The value proposition for customers in this approach is the guaranteed low price. This price isn't necessarily what gets paid at the register (a point-of-purchase price); it could also be the price paid over the lifetime of the product. Lifetime costs could include, above and beyond the immediate tangible expenditures, service (or the avoidance thereof—remember the Maytag repairman?) or trouble free customer service and support. In either event, operationally excellent (OE) firms will understand what customers really do want. To deliver that price, however, firms need to focus on streamlined and efficient processes to achieve lowest total cost. The four organizational dimensions of operational excellence are the following:

- Core processes are organized around offering a limited set of products and services. This simplifies acquisition of inputs, production processes, and training. For example, Southwest Airlines offered short-haul, point-to-point flights (no transcontinental or international flights), no checked bags, no meals, and tended to serve smaller, regional airports. This simplicity allowed them to use a single model of small and efficient planes, use small crews, and take advantage of regional airports comparative lack of traffic and congestion—all of which helped Southwest become the most efficient carrier at capital utilization. Clearly, this does

not appeal to all customers but when it does, it can be very
effective.

- OE firms tend to have a structure that is centrally controlled
with carefully planned operations. There is often little latitude
for independent decision making left to employee discretion.
High-level skills tend to be centralized.

- Management systems are typically oriented around reliable,
fast, integrated transactions. Wal-Mart is an example used by
the authors because of the way it redesigned the transaction
process from order to sale and moved toward continual replen-
ishment rather than a classic stocking inventory approach.

- The culture of the OE firm usually emphasizes efficiency and
consistency. Firms that have developed these cultures also
tend to make them egalitarian so that the ideas of frugality
and efficiency are extended through all levels. This is critical
if employees are to buy in. For instance, Nucor Steel offered
few, if any, special perks to executives (such as parking spots)
and operated company headquarters in a North Carolina
strip mall. Lincoln Electric also eliminated many hierarchical differences to develop the attention to shared efficiency.
These include no assigned parking spaces for executives and
all employees eating in the same dining room. Finally, from a
hiring perspective, OE firms want trainable people who will
buy into the company values.

Product Leadership: Providing the Best Product

The value proposition of the product leadership (PL) firm is to provide
products that push or exceed existing performance boundaries and to
keep doing it. These firms have to be agnostically creative or willing to
identify and implement good ideas whether internally or externally developed. They also have to be very fast to market, and willing to leapfrog or
cannibalize their own products before cash flows from current winners
are exhausted. For this approach, successful Product Leaders can expect
to command price premia for what they do.

- The core processes of PL firms focus on both invention *and* commercialization, whether by taking advantage of existing market opportunities or creating them. Clearly, this requires not only creative and technical product or process skills but also an equivalent commitment to skills in marketing and market development—otherwise the new product gets lost in the general background noise. A good example of how this is done is the Walt Disney Company after Michael Eisner assumed control. Eisner revitalized the animated film division with releases like *The Little Mermaid*, *Aladdin*, and *The Lion King*. Among other issues, Eisner invested $30 million in a new computer animated production system that helped cut the development cycle time for animated features from 4 or 5 years to 12 to 18 months.[10] Further, Disney aggressively developed new marketing approaches, such as the trailer for *The Lion King*, which was the first 12 minutes of the film; built strong internal coordination across divisions by introducing new characters to division heads to facilitate exploitation of the characters in multiple venues; and coordinated licensing opportunities with external partners like Burger King or Mattel.[11]

- The structure of PL firms tends toward the loosely structured organization, often with temporary, project-driven structures. In contrast to OE firms where skills are usually concentrated in central positions, in PL firms they are evident throughout the organization. In this project-based environment, managers organize around intermediate milestones and outcomes on tight deadlines.

- Management systems are oriented around results in new product success. The idea is to maintain an appropriately risk-oriented frame of mind—to reward experimentation and not punish failure (as long as it is clear lessons from failure are learned and applied).

- PL cultures value and encourage accomplishment, imagination, and creativity. From a recruiting and selection point of view, this can mean a focus on the unconventional thinker if not outright mavericks. This can be very difficult to do as it calls for hiring people you may not like or that you believe will not fit well in your firm—yet it is these characteristics that provide the needed innovation and creativity.[12]

Customer Intimacy: Providing the Integrated Solution

The value proposition for firms pursuing excellence in customer intimacy (CI) is that they can provide customers with more than just product or a salable service. Rather, they focus on the total needs of the customer to provide the best total solution. This works best for customers who don't know what they really need—or are addressing symptoms rather than underlying causes. Thus, CI firms need to be able to diagnose needs and deliver results, which often entails much more than core products or services. Often, training, customization, service, or creative purchasing and financing might be involved. This means that CI firms have to be very selective about customers: Pure transaction oriented customers are not wanted because they can cut out the proposed value. What pays is a longer term, very engaged relationship in which the client retains some dependence on the skills and knowledge of the CI firm. The value for the CI firm is the premium it can charge for a package of goods and services.

- The process focus is on identifying suitable customer candidates and developing them. That is, CU firms help the customer learn what the real problem is and what the solution should be. Further, CI firms invest in getting the solution delivered properly through production and service groups that are client driven rather than, say, technology driven. IBM (already referred to in chapter 6 and used as an example by Treacy and Wiersema) is one of the best historic examples. In his history of IBM, Kevin Maney quotes technology historian Stan Augarten on the differences in approach:

> When a team of IBM salesmen called on a customer, they worked hard to show how the installation of an IBM computer would get the payroll out faster, keep better track of sales, boost efficiency, and save money.
>
> When a group of UNIVAC salesmen visited a client, however, they tended to harp on technological

matters—mercury delay lines, decimal versus binary computation—that went right over the heads of their customers, who were chiefly interested in the answer to one question: What will a computer do for me?[13]

- The structure of CI firms pushes decision making down to the employees closest to the customer. Obviously, this can be a risk, but the argument is that no one knows better than the person in the field (and that person will possess high-level skills) as to what will keep the client. In addition, the physical structure of the CI firm will often be different with representatives sharing business space with the client so as to provide superior service.
- Management systems are oriented around developing and maintaining satisfaction in a small set of carefully selected clients. The important metric is share of that customer's relevant expenditures and retention.
- The CI culture values behaviors that lead to customer satisfaction and strong relationships rather than strict (short-term) sales and revenues. As always, selection for the right personalities and attributes will be key, but even more important is the training that creates the expertise the customer needs.

Mintzberg's Critique of Strategy

There are some criticisms of this analysis, planning, investment, and structuring approach. One issue that critics (particularly Henry Mintzberg)[14] have of this planning approach is that it makes the assumption that there really is a choice for managers. Do managers really choose a "best" way or are they constrained by past decisions and are merely validating them with the current plan? This is the crux of the strategy as planning problem: Strategic investments are often long term and they definitely affect organizational structure and processes (think about the investments and commitments that have been made). However, to the extent that the environment or market or completion doesn't play along with expectations, it may be hard to change directions. It is costly to stop or reverse strategic trajectories and managers might also have prestige, firm tradition, and other (nonstrategic) issues wrapped up in the decision. Thus, once managers start down a particular strategic path, it is not clear that they really choose strategies later—they just endorse prior decisions.

Another critique from Mintzberg is concerned with the real-world problem of *thinking* versus *learning* where thinking implies that the strategic problem can be rationally approached and all relevant knowledge gathered before making the decisions. Learning implies that conditions reveal themselves or change forms over time. Mintzberg questions, in particular, the validity of possessing really adequate knowledge in advance. This has several implications. First, differences between the world that's envisioned in the plan and the world as it eventually comes to be realized leads to gaps in and failure of implementation of the strategy. Managers are scrambling to be effective based on current knowledge, even if that means varying from the formal idea. The second problem is that this sort of a priori planning might ignore what he terms "emergent" strategy or the way that managers sometimes find a real and strong pattern in what they do that was not explicitly anticipated. This often comes from success in solving immediate but recurring problems. For example, it is doubtful that Sam Walton envisioned the efficient organization Wal-Mart was to become in the late 1960s when he tried to solve the delivery and inventory problems that his stores in small towns faced. The distribution center (and subsequent changes in inventory management, cross docking, etc.) was a solution to an immediate problem that eventually became institutionalized as strategy.

These are powerful criticisms, yet the core ideas of strategic thinking remain. The three models you read about in this chapter are useful ways of organizing a theory or story of what to do (and there are more!). The most important takeaway is that effective strategies will be internally consistent in aligning objectives, investments, and context. This is where the mindful approach becomes important: It is not enough to just create a strategy, but you also have to keep paying attention to what is happening in the world and reflecting on whether the assumptions that drove your particular strategic choices are still accurate and relevant. Then, strategy becomes dynamic.

Summary

After reading about these three theories of strategic types or approaches, you've probably figured out that while they are not identical by any means, they share a number of similarities. For example, Porter's Cost Leader is much the same as Miles and Snow's Defender and Treacy and Wiersema's Operationally Excellent firms. Similarly, Prospectors look much like Product Leaders. That's useful because it means there is a lot of consistency across classification structures—which means the choice of approaches will be somewhat easier.

The two really important outcomes of these approaches are these: First, note how each scheme calls for an *internally consistent set of decisions*. To be a Cost Leader or an Analyzer or a Customer Intimate firm requires specific and interconnected sorts of resources, skills, and capabilities. Strategy is a set of investments and commitments that presumably leads to above-average performance, but without structure or consistency, these can be opportunistic, reactive, and disjointed. That will not serve you and does not amount to any kind of strategy. Thus, you have to make sure you understand the scope of the strategy (Whom will you serve? What do they want or need?) and how you are going to do this. Practically speaking, this is often an iterative process of narrowing down and more closely matching customer sets with skills and resources, both in hand and desired. At the end, what you want is clear and consistent definitions of all the components.

The second outcome is to understand that these are not short-term solutions if you do not already find yourself as a clear example of a type. For example, in both the Miles and Snow and Treacy and Wiersema models significant attention is paid to the cultures around each type. Culture takes years to build or shift because deep-seated beliefs and values have to change, and this is usually quite difficult. Even more difficult, sometimes, is changing upper management's real values: Will they stick to a strategic vision, such as PL, if a quick sale can be had at a deep discount? Signals that the strategy is just lip service erode the effectiveness very quickly!

Finally, note how each of these models can act as the binding mechanism discussed earlier in the chapter. When it is developed and communicated well, and when the organizational structures, culture, compensation, and processes are aligned with it, strategy provides a lens on the world for members of an organization that reduces uncertainty and makes their jobs easier.

CHAPTER 8

Strategic Positions for Volatile Industries

Introduction

In the last chapter, you learned about possibilities or options in the range of strategic choice. The goal of choosing a strategic position is to make investments and decisions that will align your firm with the environment and the opportunities—a sort of fine tuning for best performance. However, when industries are changing rapidly, the ideas of alignment or fit may not be so meaningful: Can you achieve fit with a moving target with investments and commitments that take time to be effective? To the extent that strategic investments tend to be long term and difficult to reverse, volatility and change complicate your decisions, increase your risks, and may limit your effective range of action.

Consider the nature of a product or industry life cycle. Figure 8.1 shows the typical course of events. When an industry emerges (or, equivalently, a new product-market does), the volume of product adoptions tends to be low. There are often many firms—usually small—seeking to identify the salient buyer needs or purchase drivers. Over time customer choices about what works and what doesn't (i.e., what they'll actually buy) pushes the designs firms produce toward the features and benefits most consumers want. Adoptions or purchases begin to accelerate quite rapidly. This is the growth phase of industry life, and in this stage competing product designs converge to a dominant design.[1] This means that most firms in the industry are producing the same sort of solution. It also means that since the products are converging in features, other buyer needs, such as price, assume more importance, which will drive marginal- or high-cost producers out of the market. As an example, the early days

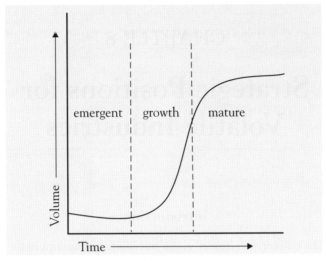

Figure 8.1. Stages in industry life cycle.

of the automotive industry were characterized by competition between three technologies: electric, steam, and internal combustion engines. Obviously, the internal combustion engine won the design battle, and for nearly a century there have been no significant producers of steam or electrical vehicles (though that appears to be changing!). Moreover, the industry has historically seen a steady consolidation as small, cost-hampered producers are bought out or driven out. Industry maturity is reached when the growth curve turns over and slows.

According to researchers, strategic choice likely reflects this evolution. In young industries, few firms want to commit resources to competing on efficiency or cost leadership (through costly investment in produc-tion) when volumes are low and it is not clear what the right or winning technology will be. What is the right strategy here? At the mature end of the cycle, the opposite is true: There are usually fewer, larger firms operat-ing in an environment where needs are well defined. What strategy makes the most sense now?

In this chapter, you'll learn about the merit of life cycle: strategy choice recommendations as well as what works when conditions are even more extreme. That is, the industry life cycle described earlier can be inter-rupted by catastrophic events; by fundamental changes in the regulatory environment, which are sometimes called discontinuous or punctuated equilibrium problems; and by evolutionary changes that are more continuous. In some industries, product life cycles plunge to mere months, which means producers have to pick the right new product very often. In others, the technological underpinnings on the supply side are shifting or even emerging: Uncertainty and the price of entry are high, and the cost of choosing the wrong platform is often failure. How then do managers choose? In this chapter, you'll read about ways to discern if your industry is, in fact, volatile; reasons why such industry level changes occur; and some strategies for managing in those environments.

Your Industry May Be Volatile If . . .

Since all industries experience change to some degree or another, how would you know if your firm competes in an industry that is considered volatile or rapidly changing? In this section, we'll look at some classifications and measures of change rate.

One sort of industry volatility is technological in origin.[2] Technological changes can occur upstream (as a supply issue), in the industry (as a dominant design issue), and between the industry and its customers (as an intermediating issue). Technological change can be measured in many ways, such as patents, but industries vary in how firms create and protect intellectual property, making assessment a bit more difficult. Nonetheless, the following are some indicators.

As noted earlier, industries in the early stages of development or industry life cycle tend to have more and smaller firms experimenting with product designs and features. All else equal, emerging industries are more volatile than mature industries. Relatedly, you can assess the number of competing technologies vying to solve the same problem[3] because if there are several, your industry is in the period before a dominant design emerges and therefore reasonably early in the cycle.

The rate of innovation can also be a good indicator. In some, but not all, industries, patents are the preferred way to protect new intellectual property. Research indicates that the higher the patent rate (filing and granting), the more firms alter production inputs, changing how they solve the fundamental economic problem.[4] While there are databases and reports you can purchase that will give this information on all industries, you can begin preliminary investigations through the United States

Patent and Trademark Office (USPTO) website. The USPTO carries years of data on product and process patents organized by technological similarity.[5] Likely, you'll also need to understand the classification system and note that firms in your industry might be active in two or more classes. With this, you can assess the absolute number of patents being granted in an industry and the rate of change in patenting, both of which can be useful indicators.

A limitation to these counts is that industries vary in the extent to which member firms use patents as the primary means of intellectual property protection. For instance, research shows that patenting is very important in the pharmaceutical, chemical, and petroleum industries but less so in industries like automobiles or office equipment.[6] Partially, this may be because patents in such industries can be more easily invented around or subverted. Thus, an alternative measure is based on the new product development cycle for your industry or how the rate of new product introductions changes.

The basic idea here is that the shorter the life cycle of products, the more that firms in an industry need to invest in new product extensions and, as a riskier move, platforms or completely new product directions. The length of product life cycles (and, really, what you are interested in is the "half life" as new work is being done to replace those aging products) can be estimated as the duration between introduction and removal from the product catalog or offering. The product life cycle and the share of industry revenues from new products can be used to distinguish between fast and slow cycle industries. Fast cycle or fast clockspeed industries have much shorter product cycles and generate a larger portion of total revenues from those new introductions. Examples of such industries include computers, semiconductors, fashion clothing, cell phones, and toys while slow cycle industries include construction, automobile, and aircraft production.[7] Note that product complexity is often a barrier to short product cycles because more components or modules need to be properly and reliably integrated, the assurance of which is time consuming. Fast cycle industries are clearly more volatile because the basis for competition keeps changing in unpredictable ways.

Another measure of volatility (called market volatility[8]) is in how revenue streams for industries change. Volatile industries might exhibit significant changes in total industry revenues in either direction with an annual 10% change offered as a boundary between stable and volatile.[9] Other market-based measures include firm entry and exit rates as well as acquisition and merger activity. In these latter measures, you should be interested in both an absolute level and the change in rates. For example, the U.S. brewing industry, until about 1990, had experienced increasing maturity and consolidation such that the number of brewers had dropped to about 50. However, for reasons we'll explore in the next section, microbrewing became a feasible strategy and the number of entrants ran into the thousands. Certainly, these were by definition small firms and many of them failed, but they do illustrate a fundamental shift in the stability of the industry.

What Causes Industry Change and Turbulence?

Anita McGahan has developed a useful framework for assessing issues in industry change, evolution, and obsolescence.[10] She argues that two sorts of challenges emerge: Threats of obsolescence to *core activities* (what industry firms do to provide value to customers—i.e., how they solve the problem) and threats of obsolescence to *core assets* (which is more of a firm level problem, but not exclusively). From these, four types of industry change are derived.

Because they attack how the industry problem is solved, *threats to core activities* are an industry wide problem. Here are some sources:

Environmental change or changes at the PEST level can render current industry solutions valueless or change the rules for determining why they are valuable. (Donald Sull calls these "sudden death threats"[11]). For example, *changes in regulation* (a P, or political, shift) can attack activities in competition-constraining or competition-enhancing ways. Some changes impair or destroy what industry firms do: When the U.S. government imposed Prohibition in 1919, the effect on alcohol producers was obvious and dramatic, forcing a switch to other sources of revenue. The Jim Beam distillers turned to rock quarrying and fruit farming while brewers entered industries as diverse as production of baking yeast or ice cream, shipping, and real estate. Ultimately and not unexpectedly, the attrition rate in these industries was very high.

Alternatively, some changes can encourage competition or make it easier to enter and compete. One example is the deregulation of the U.S.

air carrier industry in the late 1970s, which led to many new entrants and the failure of legacy carriers in relatively short order. An even more recent example is what happened after the telecom industry was deregulated in 1996. This very quickly led to the convergence of the networking products industry (firms like Cisco or Bay Networks) with the telecommunications industry (firms such as Nortel, Alcatel, etc.). Combined with the deployment of Internet technologies, this change in regulation led to an enormous surge in new entrants, mergers, acquisitions, and failures. This was an exceedingly volatile period in that industry's history.

Another source of change is in *sociocultural values*. Consider how the evolving social attitudes toward tobacco usage, animal furs in clothing, or consumption of meat products or alcohol has affected their respective industries. In all cases, consumption in the United States and Europe has been decreasing and will likely do so in the future because these tend to reflect fundamental shifts in values and beliefs about a "right" life.

Demand and supply shifts can also cause turbulence. The Great Recession of 2008–2010 (like all recessions) has had an adverse effect on luxury goods makers. Even though the affluent often continue to purchase such goods, the aspirational or nearly-as-affluent segment that tends to buy up in good times does not do so in recessions. The price-to-value relationship has been eroded.

Fundamental *technological shifts* can create newly important substitutes from innovation occurring outside (usually) the core industry. This makes what focal industry firms do irrelevant (or less relevant) because the demand for those activities has disappeared. For instance, the web has broadly decreased the value created by auto dealerships. Because gathering information was costly to consumers (How far would you go to get comparative prices on a new car?), dealers were able to control prices and command higher prices. The advent of various information sites such as Kelley Blue Book or Edmunds.com have made price shopping much easier and pricing much more uniform. Dealers have been cut out of the pricing system and increasingly function as supply and service depots.

Threats of obsolescence to *core assets* challenge how firms do their own value adding activities. This happens within an industry (not just to the industry). That is, the core resources, knowledge, and brand capital that have previously been deployed can be affected. This is a firm level issue, but note that if a number of firms have similar resource or asset profiles, the challenge can be broadly disruptive. Patent expiration in the pharmaceutical industry is an illustration of how industry structures can shift. Patents in this industry mean more here than in other industries because of the drug approval process that new treatments have to go through, but when the patent for a drug expires, generics usually flood the market. If the drugs in question are blockbusters or major sellers, a real shift in industry structure can result. Thus, because the number one and two prescription drugs in the United States (Pfizer's Lipitor with sales of $11.2 billion in 2009 and Bristol-Myers Squibb's Plavix with 2009 sales of $9.5 billion[12]) are going off patent in 2011, the prospects for upheaval in the industry are high.

McGahan also notes that challenges to core assets are often the outcome of buyers acquiring new, better, or just more knowledge from the emergence of a superior marketplace of ideas. When people are better-informed buyers, those who specialized in previously abstruse information have less value. Further, innovation within the industry, which unlike the emergence of substitutes described earlier implies evolutionary changes to how the industry firms solve customer problems, can challenge the assets of some but not all firms. An example used earlier in chapter 2 dealt with the changes in how the bookselling industry has evolved. A more detailed example comes from the changes in the American brewing industry and the rise of microbrews where a once very stable industry has suddenly become quite dynamic.

The explosive growth in the number of firms in the brewing industry was described earlier—but what caused it? There are likely a number of contributors. First, regulatory change set the stage. In 1978, President Carter repealed a regulatory artifact from the end of Prohibition that outlawed home brewing. The repeal spawned a tremendous growth in the hobby as brewers could now acquire malted grains, yeast, and hops that let them create or replicate beer styles that were not possible to purchase. The skills that many home brewers developed in the garage or basement provided the technical foundation for the next step: commercial brewing. Fairly quickly, two home brewers—Ken Grossman and Paul Camusi—started up Sierra Nevada Brewing Co., which not only survived but ranked in 2009 as one of the top 10 brewers in the United States.

Second, there were some shifts in customer preferences and demand. American beers had been converging for decades toward a style called the American standard lager, a relatively light, effervescent brew. By the 1980s, this was virtually the only domestic style available, and while it was very uniform in terms of production and quality control, an increasing number of consumers found it deficient in flavor and aroma compared to other styles of beer. And, these consumers knew this because local markets were increasingly open to higher priced beers from Europe.

A related but even broader demand shift—the emergence of "lifestyle" based consumption in the '70s and '80s—was another driver of the craft brewing movement. This period saw the emergence of the educated class or the white collar meritocracy. The first great bump of baby boomers graduated college in the 1970s. Their embrace of and engagement in the concurrent growth of information technology as well as the shift away from manufacturing employment has meant the emergence of a large number of the well educated and well compensated workers. This led to a certain style of consumption. This educated class rejected conspicuous consumption of luxuries, such as boats or furs, but embraced spending a great deal for necessities (though at a very high end) and a cultivated appreciation of uncommon versions of commonplace goods such as coffee, building materials, water, and so on. Brooks describes the ethos as one focusing on the "authentic, natural, warm, rustic, simple, honest, organic, comfortable, craftsmanlike, unique, sensible, [and] sincere."[13] Thus, we have seen the emergence or resurgence of firms like Starbucks, Republic of Tea, Viking, Whole Foods, and so on.

These purchasing patterns readily extend to beer, particularly with respect to local breweries as an alternative to the uniform products of megabreweries. Early on, this manifested as a growth in import beer sales in the early 1980s. While this has persisted, the real growth has been in the conscious consumption of locally and regionally produced beers that emphasize either a resurrection of old styles of beer, such as ales, porters, stouts, lambics, and the like, or particularly American interpretations of these styles, such as American pale and pumpkin ales and rye and chili beers. As an illustration of this growth, the Beer Advocate website lists reviews of more than 13,000 labels in its American Ale section.[14]

Collectively, these changes in the environment upset a very mature and stable industry. There was likely little attack on the core activities of the older incumbents (brewing is still brewing), but the threat to core assets, such as reputation and brand image, of most of the larger firms has been intense. In fact, while overall sales in the industry have been flat, growth in the microbrew or craft segment has been robust—which means that the historic incumbents have been watching revenue and share drop.

In a general sense, these threats can be combined to describe four types of change trajectory but from an industry-wide perspective, two are of most interest. These are *radical* change (when both assets and activities are threatened) and *intermediating* change (when activities are threatened but assets are not). An excellent example of radical industry change is what happened in the computing industry in the 1970s–1990s. Consider the transition from mainframe to minicomputing. This represented a challenge to activities and assets on many levels. First, the old mainframe model focused on large customers, such as governmental agencies, banks, insurance companies, and the like, which all shared similar sorts of computing problems. The solution was centralized and large-scale computing that served a relative few customers. However, advances in integrated chips reduced the cost and increased the efficiency of computing, which made smaller architectures (such as mini and then PC based platforms) possible. These solved smaller problems such as engineers and architects adopting small office minicomputers in the 1970s from Digital Electronics Corporation (DEC) and Data General for drafting and project management. The challenges to core activities for mainframe makers was quite clear, but what about core assets? Most of the mainframe firms (and particularly IBM) focused on overall problem solving through direct sales engineering. This is a version of Treacy and Wiersema's CI model, but recall that this requires that the industry firm create and maintain a certain dependency by the customer. However, the emergence of new computing architectures and information about them educated potential customers, attacking the value proposition.

Intermediating change takes industry players out of their central role. Aside from what happened in the brewing industry, an interesting example comes from the shaving industry. Before King Gillette, men shaved themselves with straightedge (or cutthroat) razors, or more frequently they patronized barbershops. Even those who shaved themselves faced the problem of caring for and properly sharpening the razor. Gillette's invention of the safety razor at the turn of the 20th century about killed barbering as an industry because the core activities—the knowledge and skill that barbers had to shave customers with a straight razor—was captured in a technological shift. Curiously enough, the Internet has spawned a renaissance in and return to older styles of shaving as a rejection of the current dominant designs in razors—including Gillette's!

What to Do in Turbulent Industries

As you've seen, when change rates and uncertainty in an industry are high, it is likely an error to make a large bet—that is, strategic investments—on a particular outcome because the price of failure or guessing wrong can be crippling, if not fatal. This is why strategy researchers in this area often advise a policy of *active waiting* or investing to improvise and respond. Donald Sull describes this as first, keep the vision fuzzy but the priorities (short- and medium-term goals in operating or market results) clear.[15]

Similarly, Shona Brown and Kathleen Eisenhardt argue that in highly volatile industry environments, adopting a strategic process between rigid planning or investing in a particular version of the future and pure reaction to market forces can be effective.[16] When change rates are high, it is unclear what demand will be. In their analysis of technology firms, Brown and Eisenhardt found that the more successful firms stayed on top of the changes using four future probing mechanisms: experimental products or line extensions, alliances with customers, appointing staff whose responsibility was to act as "futurists," and facilitating (and expecting) extensive communication between project groups. To this, Sull adds the recommendation of a good cash position or war chest for rapid action when opportunity presents.

Experimental product probes are designed to identify new opportunities and how markets might shape up. These are designed to be low-cost product experiments, such as extensions to or new options in existing product lines intended for new markets. Probes can also be rudimentary or "quick and dirty" approaches that just test a perceived opportunity for customer acceptance. The virtues of this approach are that it is usually fast (the technological core is often in place) and usually doesn't require the resources for development that larger-scale projects do. In addition, because they are low cost, failure isn't as significant. In fact, failure can provide valuable learning.

Alliances with certain kinds of customers can also form a probe, provided the customers are *not* mainstream. Mainstream partners can be exceedingly valuable, but they likely won't give you the insight into what's new that you'll need. The right partners here are those suppliers and customers whose needs are underserved by the industry and perhaps not even understood. We can use the information and telecommunications (ITC) industry as a good example. Technological change in this industry has been incredibly rapid and diverse for two decades, and the problem that all firms face is that not one of them is a master of all knowledge domains. Nor is it even desirable to be so as the cost of competence (through R&D investments) is exceedingly high, given that many emerging technologies never make it to market. Another limiting factor is that learning takes time, and the pace of innovation limits how much a firm's intellectual talent can absorb and integrate. Time is too short to own it all.

Increasingly, alliances in this industry are used as way to cope. First, transitory alliances are designed to quickly tap and combine partner knowledge with the firm's own knowledge base as a probe. These are fast to build, fast to kill alliances that focus on the very near term through experimentation with joint technologies.[17] Second, firms can use alliances to keep a watchful eye on emerging technologies. In the ITC industry, most of the major players, such as Cisco, Intel, Nokia, Alcatel, and Lucent, have operated what amount to venture capital funds. These firms take equity positions in small startups developing new technology. Obviously, these technologies often fail, so full-scale investment in them by the larger incumbents is probably premature. However, the equity stake gives the investor the right to observe the technology closely and learn and, if it looks very promising, to move on with acquisition of the startup, its technology, and the technology developers.[18] A third way firms in this industry use alliances is to control some of the uncertainty of picking winning products through managing how technological standards emerge. Most standardization efforts are accompanied by, if not directed by, multilateral associations of firms organized to develop testing and interoperability expectations. This not only expedites the standardization process but also defines at earlier and earlier stages which technologies will succeed.[19]

Futurists are, as mentioned in chapter 3, people who have made a study of how trends emerge and what they mean. Brown and Eisenhardt argue that more successful firms attend to and encourage internal experts with skills in both the technological base and the associated markets to form evolving projections. Obviously, reading the future often misses.

Just think of IBM president Tom Watson, Jr.'s reputed observation in 1947 that there was a world market for perhaps five computers or DEC president Ken Olson arguing in 1977 that no one would ever want a computer in the home! Nonetheless, these projections can provide the basis of active conversation and debate and provide the roadmap for the reconnaissance and alliances described earlier.

Alternatively, some firms use scenario planning as a probing mechanism. Scenario development is a semi to very formal way of asking and answering, "What happens if . . . ?" The purpose is to identify key future change factors such as environmental issues or political conditions, assess how they could change, construct models that link the change factors (as in cause and effect linkages or issues centered around a common theme), and assess the implications of the scenarios that result when variables change (i.e., is the difference slight or significant?).[20] In a sense, this is quite similar to the work you've already done in PEST and industry analysis. The difference here is that you want to be stretching yourself to consider not just likely changes but also the strange and unlikely.[21] A well-known example is that of Royal Dutch/Shell in the early 1970s and how they identified, among other issues that could happen, the rise of OPEC and subsequent disruptions to petroleum production. The point is not that this was predicted—it was not—but that Shell managers had already anticipated how they would respond *if* it happened (and they did so quite effectively).[22]

These firms are also serious about extensive internal communication. This can be formal, as in structured, scheduled meetings or less so as in consistent, within-project discussion. Even more important is idea- and insight-sharing across product or project groups where the "not invented here" syndrome is explicitly rejected. New ideas and approaches (and the lessons of failure) are disseminated quickly.

Finally, successful firms in these industries have accumulated cash or capital reserves to be able to move when opportunities present themselves.

Summary

Commitment to a strategic direction is intended to provide internal consistency in investments, processes, and governance mechanisms. Some will argue this all goes out the window (and is therefore meaningless) when industries are chaotic, uncertain, or turbulent. It is true that under such conditions, it is much more difficult to be confident about choices, and as you've already seen, long term investments in a specific direction can be ill-advised. This does not mean that you are paralyzed, though!

If you'll reflect on the sorts of strategies discussed in the last chapter, you'll likely recognize that a number of them are perfectly adaptable to these sorts of environments. To reiterate some points made earlier, when technologies and customer choices are evolving and unclear, making a commitment to efficiency or cost leadership type strategies is hazardous. These typically require substantial investment in specialized capital that requires relatively long production runs to reduce costs. If the solutions wanted by customers change and the specialized equipment isn't adaptable, the investment is lost or obsolete. That can be fatal! On the other hand, strategies like the prospector from Miles and Snow or the PL and even the CI approaches from Treacy and Wiersema are quite consistent with what has been discussed as successful practices in this chapter. Recall how these strategies emphasize flexibility, creativity, and dynamic responsiveness. Structures and processes such as job shop environments, experimentation, organization around projects, and fluid reporting structures are what support the adaptive objectives of probing, alliance, and communication. Thus, turbulence can moderate your choices, but there are still solid choices to be made.

CHAPTER 9

Some Final Thoughts on Practice and Improvisation

Form a conceptual point of view, developing a strategy for your firm is really pretty straightforward. Constantinos Markides[1] argues that a strategic position can be summed up as the responses to three simple questions:

- Who are my customers—and who are not?
- What will I offer customers—and what will I not offer?
- How should I do this in the most efficient way?

You'll recall that these are basically the same as the founding questions in chapter 7, which dealt with choosing or formulating a strategy for your firm. The questions are simple but turn out to be quite difficult to answer clearly, especially if you have no way to attack them. Developing good analytic techniques is a powerful position from which to answer, at least in part, those questions.

However, in working with students and executives (particularly the latter, who have often been tasked with the job), I hear strategic analysis and planning criticized because they say it is difficult and because even when pursued, it doesn't work. Yet, I hope you see that analysis and planning is important because it can do the following:

- Guide your significant—that is, strategic—investments and commitments
- Provide a platform for contribution by others, which makes more hands for crafting and influencing the strategy
- Bind the members of the organization together and provide a common basis for action

The general purpose of this book is to specifically address the first criticism and to point to a way to deal with the second. In general, I agree that the analysis process can be frustrating and confusing when the tools are unfamiliar. Yet, in these past chapters, you've worked through a large set of well-known and proven techniques and seen how and why they are applied. Your work with the very general environmental assessment model (PEST), industry analysis (five forces), and firm level techniques applicable to your own organization and competitors (VRIN [Valuable, Rare, Inimitable, and Nonsubstitutable] model) should resolve one aspect of unfamiliarity: understanding which tools to use and when to apply them.

There is little doubt, however, that the first time you work through an entire analysis cycle, this will be difficult to do. First, you will need to find the right information or, if and when it doesn't exist in an easily accessible form, develop synthesis and workarounds. Synthesis comes from combining and analyzing data sources to create a new source, which can be exceedingly valuable. Even so, you may have to deal with less than complete data, at least for the time being. That is not what you want, but you can move forward if you note it and think about variances in what you initially estimate might do to your work—and remember to keep pursuing the right data.

Another issue is that you will likely find your definitions and boundaries changing over the course of the work. You might not know it is happening, but it can show up when a conclusion you reach at one stage contradicts an earlier conclusion. This is actually quite a useful discovery: You've either erred in one or the other conclusions or you've changed the basis for analysis, which permits contradictions to exist. Both are fixable if you pay attention to them.

Both of these factors lead to an important third reason that analysis is difficult: Practitioners usually don't do it often enough to gain proficiency and this can lead to frustration. An illustration: I play golf, in a sense. I own the right tools (clubs, shoes, bag), I understand what I'm trying to do (get the ball in the cup), and several times a year I'll walk a course with my tools and my understanding. You can likely imagine the results because you see the fundamental problem: Doing well at golf or anything complex requires practice and application, and I'm not doing that. The same is true of strategic analysis. Subsequent passes through the process will be faster, easier, and more effective because you don't have to create sources—you review and revise. Certainly, you will need to revisit your assumptions and your conclusions to roll in new information and eliminate the obsolete and attend to changes in industry boundaries and competitors. But, in many ways the first time through makes the second and third and so on far easier. Persistence and consistency are critical to the reliability of your work.

The second primary criticism—that doing strategic analysis is not useful since it doesn't work—is more difficult to address because I think there are several reasons why people adopt this perspective.

First, it has been a distressingly common practice to deintegrate the planning (or analysis and formulation) stage and the execution stages of strategy.[2] The planning process, often undertaken by senior executives, generates a document that is then turned over to lower-level executives to turn into results. Obviously, this destroys the context of the analytic conclusion for those implementing managers: They see *what* to do but not *why*. Moreover, the day-to-day demands of business and the manager's functional responsibilities often get in the way of recreating the reasoning that led to the plan. If these managers run into situations that are not identical to those envisioned in the plan, the prescribed actions become pointless or futile—and managers see this. The strategy is a waste of their time and scarce resources that, they reason, could be better used elsewhere, so the implementation was cursory.

The second and even greater contributing cause of perceived irrelevance is that strategy and strategic analysis is often approached as something that ought to be done but as infrequently as possible. This arises because strategy is often regarded as the purview of the CEO and, to some extent, the senior management team. Thus, strategy is often regarded as "not my job" and as an imposition because of it. I suspect the origin of this is the common approach that renders strategy-making an episodic—if not spasmodic—effort. This approach also invokes the problem of unfamiliarity discussed previously. That's why the idea of strategic analysis, implementation, and assessment is much more effectively approached as a *cyclical, ongoing process* (Figure 9.1)—a process that persists and becomes part of the fabric of the firm. This has several advantages.

First, keeping up to date with the analytics and the assessment requires that the job be broadly shared. The crafting of decisions about what to do and why can get distributed to many more managers and staff.

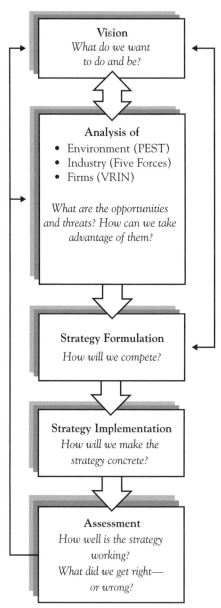

Figure 9.1. The strategy cycle.

The cognitive sharing takes the burden off the previously few involved. Second, continuous strategy can eliminate the problem of the disjunction between formulation and implementation. Now, staff at many levels understands how and why the strategy is what it is, what events might mean for that strategy, and what to do about it. Henry Mintzberg observes that by creating the right systems to encourage and stimulate participation, you get engagement in strategy.[3] This may not solve the problem of "right strategy" in the sense that broad engagement automatically makes everything work to plan, but it can improve the probability of acceptable outcomes and thus improve the quality of the feedback for subsequent efforts.

Another way of thinking about the level of intellectual investment needed is through a metaphor for what happens in the give and take of ideas and information in the analytic process. Sometimes, especially early on in the learning process, students get frustrated because they feel they can't go "outside the box," and I tell them they are correct—because they aren't ready. To illustrate this, I show them a video of Gabriela Montero and her approach to Mozart's 20th Piano Concerto[4] because, even more than sports, jazz and improvisation have become popular metaphors for what happens (or should happen) with strategy.[5] Jazz works because it is adaptive and creative yet founded in disciplined pursuit of mastery. Improvisation requires individual skills yet is fundamentally a group effort, emphasizing attentive listening and "self-reflectivity"[6] or the ability to avoid self-indulgent and destructive dissonance.

Researchers who use this metaphor tend to focus on the listening, openness, and communication elements because they translate directly to how people might more effectively relate to each other. They are certainly important but for our purposes, the metaphor is even more powerful because of what is required to get to that improvisational point. Before a musician can improvise effectively, he must first master an instrument well enough that when performing he is not thinking about the technical elements of playing it but rather letting the music play through. Further, a musician needs to understand the musical genre, its grammar and vocabulary, and its influential interpreters and their approaches. Jazz pieces, for instance, have a language or structure (and maybe several dialects) that usually includes an introduction of a theme, exposition of the theme or main melody, recapitulation, and coda or tag.[7] Even then, what masters do within the structure teaches as well: Marc Sabatella cites Clark Terry, a well known trumpet and flugelhorn player, who described this part of the process as "imitate, assimilate, innovate."[7] You can't improvise easily unless and until you've paid your (learning) dues. Finally, the musician needs to understand the song itself and how to fit into it. In short, the ability to improvise requires a substantial investment in basic skills before the more social issues of communication, reflexivity, and the like come into play. Thinking outside the box requires first that you know the *interior* of the box very, very well—or what results is just noise!

Jazz is a good metaphor here because it captures the sense of dynamics and responsiveness that a well-functioning strategic process embodies. I sincerely believe that the skills you have learned here are equivalent to the technical skills musicians develop, that the language and grammar of your industry can be mastered, and that with them you can not only be comfortable and competent in analysis when your environment is stable but also be ready to improvise when needed. Practice, persistence, and process take your work beyond a mere exercise—it becomes a powerful way of interpreting and interacting with your world.

Notes

Chapter 1

1. Mintzberg (1990).
2. Jackson (2001a).
3. Jackson (2001b).
4. Christensen and Raynor (2003).
5. "Fortune 500: 1958" (2010).
6. "Fortune 500: 2008" (2010).
7. Montgomery (2008), p. 58.
8. Carton and Hofer (2006).

Chapter 2

1. Zahra and Chaples (1993).
2. Porac and Thomas (1994).
3. Dosi (1988).
4. Bradley, Ghemawat, and Foley (2002); Ghemawat (2007).
5. Joseph (2009); "Ranking" (2009).
6. WardsAuto.com (2010)
7. Edmunds.com (2010).
8. Tremblay and Tremblay (2005).
9. "A mixed forecast for beer" (2006).

Chapter 3

1. Edwards and Satariano (2010).
2. Inglehart and Baker (2001).
3. Frey (2009).
4. Allen (2009).
5. Bensinger (2009); "Update on California" (2009).
6. Conference Board (2009).
7. "U.S. interim projections" (2009).
8. Bureau of Labor Statistics (2009).
9. Carlson (2010); "Millennials" (2010).
10. Williams (1980).

11. Reitzes (1995).

12. Wilcox (2010).

13. "Who said that?" (2009).

Chapter 4

1. "Fortune 500 top industries" (2008).

2. Damodaran (2010b).

3. Damodaran (2010a).

4. Porter (1979), Porter (2008).

5. Tremblay and Tremblay (2005).

6. Clark (1996); "Assets and liabilities" (2010).

7. Ying (1990).

8. Scherer, Beckenstein, Kaufer and Murphy (1975).

9. Ghemawat and Stander, H., III (1990).

10. Ghemawat (1987, 1992).

11. Scherer et al. (1975).

12. Yoffie (2006, 2009); IBISWorld (2010).

13. Major (2005); Coffee and Palm (2005); Brown (2004).

14. "Man in the magic hat," (2001).

15. Jarvis, Rungie, and Lockshin (2007); Nicholls (2008).

16. Federal Trade Commission (2003).

17. National Aeronautics and Space Administration (NASA, 2007).

18. "How much does a liquor license cost?" (2009).

19. McGraw (2009).

20. Barney (2001).

21. Porter (1980).

Chapter 5

1. Buschena, Gray, and Severson (1998).

2. Porter (1979); Porter (2008)

3. Crawford (2009).

4. Porter (1979, 2008).

5. "U.S. economic accounts" (2010).

6. "GDP growth rate" (2010).

7. "Architect's offices" (2009).

8. "Legal services" (2009).

9. "Aircraft parts manufacturing" (2009).

10. Porter (1979), Porter (2008).

11. Porter (1998).

Chapter 6

1. "Fortune global 500" (2008).
2. Rumelt (1991).
3. Bradley et al. (2002).
4. Rumelt (1997).
5. Barney (1991).
6. Teece, Pisano, and Shuen (1997).
7. Barney (1991, 1995).
8. Ashton (2000).
9. O'Reilly and Pfeffer (1995).
10. Szulanksi (2000).
11. Heskett and Hallowell (1993, 1997).
12. Lieberman and Montgomery (1988)
13. Montgomery (1991, 1994).
14. Dierickx and Cool (1989).
15. Schrage (2002).
16. Barney (1995).
17. Heskett and Hallowell (1993, 1997).
18. Heskett and Hallowell (1993, 1997).
19. Campbell, Whitehead, and Finkelstein (2009).

Chapter 7

1. Treacy and Wiersema (1995a), p. 89.
2. Collis and Rukstad (2008).
3. Porter (1985).
4. Bradley and Ghemawat (2002).
5. Ghemawat and Stander (1992, 1998).
6. Bradley and Ghemawat (2002).
7. Womack and Jones (1994).
8. Miles and Snow (1978); Miles, Snow, Meyer, and Coleman, Jr. (1978).
9. Treacy and Wiersema (1993, 1995a, 1995b).
10. Rukstad and Collis (2001, 2009).
11. Knoop and Reavis (1998).
12. Sutton (2001).
13. Maney (2003).
14. Mintzberg (1987a, 1987b, 1990).

Chapter 8

1. Anderson and Tushman (1990).
2. Snyder and Glueck (1982).
3. Sommer (2009).
4. Basmann, McAleer, and Slottje (2007).
5. *Patent counts by class by year, part A1* (2009).
6. Mansfield (1986); Cohen, Nelson, and Walsh (2000).
7. Mendelson and Pillai (1999).
8. Snyder and Glueck (1982).
9. Anterasian, Graham, and Money (1996).
10. McGahan (2000, 2004).
11. Sull (2005).
12. Tarsala (2009).
13. Brooks (2000), p. 83.
14. "Beer styles" (2010).
15. Sull (2005).
16. Brown and Eisenhardt (1997).
17. Duysters and de Man (2003).
18. Warner, Fairbank, and Steensma (2006).
19. Warner and Fairbank (2008).
20. Walsh (2005).
21. Singer and Piluso (2009)
22. Raspin and Terjesen (2007).

Chapter 9

1. McCarthy, Markides, and Mintzberg (2000).
2. Wall and Wall (1995).
3. McCarthy (2000).
4. Montero (2008).
5. Gold and Hirshfeld (2005); Eisenhardt (1997); Dennis and Macaulay (2007); Neilson (1992).
6. Dennis and Macaulay (2007).
7. Sabatella (2000).

References

A mixed forecast for beer. (2006). *Modern Brewery Age*. Retrieved from http://www.breweryage.com/industry/

Aircraft parts manufacturing. (n.d.).Retrieved from http://premium.hoovers.com.ezaccess.libraries.psu.edu/subscribe/

Allen, M. (2009, Oct. 1). How 35.5 MPG will change our vehicles and the way we drive. *Popular Mechanics*. Retrieved from http://www.popularmechanics.com/automotive/new_cars/4320899.html

Anderson, P., & Tushman, M. (1990). Technological discontinuities and dominant designs: A cyclical model of technological change. *Administrative Science Quarterly, 35*(4), 604–633.

Anterasian, C., Graham, J., & Money, R. (1996). Are U.S. managers superstitious about market share? *Sloan Management Review, 37*(4), 67–77.

Architect's offices.(n.d.). Retrieved from http://premium.hoovers.com.ezaccess.libraries.psu.edu/subscribe/

Ashton, Z. (2000). Clinical trials and the FDA. Retrieved from http://www.fool.com/specials/2000/sp000405fda.htm

Board of Governors of the Federal Reserve System. (2010). *Assets and liabilities of commercial banks in the United States—H.8* Retrieved from http://www.federalreserve.gov/Releases/h8/20100305/

Barney, J. (1991). Firm resources and sustained competitive advantage. *Journal of Management, 17*(1), 99–120.

Barney, J. (1995). Looking inside for competitive advantage. *Academy of Management Executive, 9*(4), 49–59.

Barney, J. (2001). *Gaining and sustaining competitive advantage*. Upper Saddle River, NJ: Prentice Hall.

Bartlett, C. A., & O'Connell, J. (1998). *Lincoln Electric: Venturing abroad*. Cambridge, MA: Harvard Business Publishing.

Basmann, R., McAleer, M., & Slottje, D. (2007). Patent activity and technological change. *Journal of Econometrics, 139*(2), 355–375.

Beer styles.(n.d.). Retrieved April 17, 2010, from http://beeradvocate.com/beer/style

Bensinger, K. (2009, January 19). California emission waiver looms for automakers. *Los Angeles Times*. Retrieved from http://articles.latimes.com/2009/jan/19/business/fi-fueleconomy19

Bradley, S., Ghemawat, P., & Foley, S. (2002). *Wal-Mart Stores, Inc*. Cambridge, MA: Harvard Business Publishing.

Brooks, D. (2000). *Bobos in paradise: The new upper class and how they got here.* New York, NY: Simon & Schuster.

Brown, K. (2004). Holding onto customers. *Wireless Week, 10*(4), 6.

Brown, S., & Eisenhardt, K. (1997). The art of continuous change: Linking complexity theory and time-paced evolution in relentlessly shifting organizations. *Administrative Science Quarterly, 42*(1), 1–34.

U.S. Department of Labor, Bureau of Labor Statistics. (2007). *The 30 fastest growing occupations covered in the 2008–09 Occupational Outlook Handbook.* Retrieved from http://www.bls.gov/news.release/ooh.t01.htm

Buschena, D., Gray, R., & Severson, E. (1998). *Changing structures in the barley production and malting industries of the United States and Canada.* Montana State University Trade Research Center, Policy Issues Paper no. 8. Retrieved May 5, 2010, from http://www2.montana.edu/jantle/trc/pdf/conferences/confproc98/buschena.pdf

Campbell, A., Whitehead, J., & Finkelstein, S. (2009). Why good leaders make bad decisions. *Harvard Business Review, 87*(2), 60–66.

Carlson, E. (2009). 20th-century U.S. generations. *Population Bulletin, 64*(1). Retrieved from http://www.prb.org/Publications/PopulationBulletins/2009/20thcenturyusgenerations.aspx

Carton, B., & Hofer, C. (2006). *Measuring organizational performance: Metrics for entrepreneurship and strategic management research.* Cheltenham, UK: Edward Elgar Publishing.

Christensen, C., & Raynor, M. (2003). Why hard-nosed executives should care about management theory. *Harvard Business Review, 81*(9), 66–74.

Clark, J. (1996). Economic cost, scale efficiency, and competitive viability in banking. *Journal of Money, Credit, and Banking, 28*(3), 342–364.

Coffey, J., & Palm, G. (2005). Are new customers really more expensive? *Bank Marketing, 37*(3), 34.

Cohen, W., Nelson, R., & Walsh, J. (2000, Feb.). *Protecting their intellectual assets: Appropriability and why U.S. manufacturing firms patent (or not)* (NBER Working Paper). Retrieved from http://www.nber.org/papers/w7552.pdf

Collis, D., & Rukstad, M. (2008). Can you say what your strategy is? *Harvard Business Review, 86*(4), 82–90.

Conference Board, Inc. (2009). *The Conference Board leading economic index (LEI) for the United States and related composite indexes for May 2009.* Retrieved from http://www.conference-board.org/pdf_free/economics/bci/rainstorm.pdf

Crawford, J. (2009, March 25). Upscale grocery stores lose customers to Kroger, Wal-Mart. *St. Louis Post-Dispatch.* Retrieved from http://www.tmcnet.com/usubmit/2009/03/25/4081436.htm

Damodaran, A. (2010a). *Betas by sector.* Retrieved March 5, 2010, from http://pages.stern.nyu.edu/~adamodar/New_Home_Page/datafile/Betas.html

Damodaran, A. (2010b). Equity risk premiums (ERP): Determinants, estimation and implications—The 2010 edition. Retrieved March 5, 2010 from http://papers.ssrn.com/sol3/papers.cfm?abstract_id=1556382

Dennis, N., & Macaulay, M. (2007). "Miles ahead"—using jazz to investigate improvisation and market orientation. *European Journal of Marketing, 41*(5/6), 608–623.

DeSarbo, W., DiBenedtto, C., Song, M., & Sinha, I. (2005). Revisiting the Miles and Snow strategic framework: Uncovering interrelationships between strategic types, capabilities, environmental uncertainty, and firm performance. *Strategic Management Journal, 26*(1), 47–74.

Dierickx, I., & Cool, K. (1989). Asset stock accumulation and sustainability of competitive advantage. *Management Science, 35*(12), 1504-1511.

Dosi, G. (1988). Sources, procedures, and microeconomic effects of innovation. *Journal of Economic Literature, 26,* 1120–1171.

Duysters, G., & de Man, A. (2003). Transitory alliances: An instrument for surviving turbulent industries, *R&D Management, 33*(1), 49–58.

Edmonds.com. (n.d.). *New car prices, reviews, & specs.* Retrieved February 15, 2010, from http://www.edmunds.com/new-cars/?tid=edmunds.n.zipentry .new.1.*

Edwards, C., & Satariano, A. (2010, February 22). Electronic Arts under assault. *Business Week,* 66–67.

Eisenhardt, K. (1997). Strategic decisions and all that jazz. *Business Strategy Review, 8*(3), 1–3.

Federal Trade Commission (2003) *Slotting allowances in the retail grocery industry.* (2003). Retrieved from http://www.ftc.gov/os/2003/11/slotting allowancerpt031114.pdf

Finkelstein, S. (2005). When bad things happen to good companies: strategy failure and flawed executives. *Journal of Business Strategy, 26*(2), 19–28.

Fortune 500 top industries: Most profitable. (2008, May). *Fortune 157*(9). Retrieved from http://money.cnn.com/magazines/fortune/fortune500/2008/performers/industries/profits/

Fortune 500: 1958 (n.d.). *Fortune.* Retrieved from http://money.cnn.com/magazines/fortune/fortune500_archive/full/1958/

Fortune 500: 2008. (n.d.). *Fortune.* Retrieved from http://money.cnn.com/magazines/fortune/fortune500/2008/full_list/

Fortune global 500 2007: Industry: Pharmaceuticals. (2007). *Fortune, 156* (2) Retrieved from http://money.cnn.com/magazines/fortune/global500/2007/industries/21/1.html

Frey, T. (2009). Notes from a futurist: Trends for business in 2009 and beyond. Retrieved from http://www.cobizmag.com/articles/notes-from-a-futurist-trends -for-business-in-2009-and-beyond/

Ghemawat, P. (1992). *Adolph Coors in the brewing industry*. Cambridge, MA: Harvard Business Publishing.

Ghemawat, P. (2007). *Wal-Mart Stores discount operations*. Cambridge, MA: Harvard Business Publishing.

Ghemawat, P., & Stander, H., III. (1998). *Nucor at a crossroads*. Cambridge, MA: Harvard Business Publishing.

Gold, M., & Hirshfeld, S. (2005). The behaviors of jazz as a catalyst for strategic renewal and growth. *The Journal of Business Strategy, 26*(5), 40–47.

Heskett, J., & Hallowell, R. (1993/1997). *Southwest Airlines—1993 (A)*. Cambridge, MA: Harvard Business Publishing.

How much does a liquor license cost? (2009). Retrieved July 14, 2009, from http://www.pallx.com/faq-answers.php

Husan, R. (1997). The continuing importance of economies of scale in the automotive industry. *European Business Review, 91*(1), 38.

IBISWorld (2010) *Soft drink production in the U.S* (IBISWorld Industry Report 31211) Retrieved from IBISWorld website: http://www.ibisworld.com .ezaccess.libraries.psu.edu/industry/default.aspx?indid=284

Inglehart, R., & Baker, W. (2001, March–April). Modernization's challenge to traditional values: Who's afraid of Ronald McDonald? *The Futurist*, pp. 16–21.

Jackson, A. (2001a). The Peninsular War: The Battle of Buçaco, 27th September 1810.Retrieved from http://www.peninsularwar.org/bucaco.htm

Jackson, A. (2001b). The Peninsular War: The Lines of Torres Vedras. Retrieved from http://www.peninsularwar.org/ltv.htm

Jarvis, W., Rungie, C., & Lockshin, L. (2007). Revealed preference analysis of red wine attributes using polarization. *International Journal of Wine Business Research, 19*(2), 127–138.

Joseph, N. (2009). Hyundai-Kia overtakes Ford to become world's 4th largest automaker. Retrieved from http://www.autoblog.com/2009/08/18/ hyundai-kia-overtakes-ford-as-worlds-4th-largest-automaker/

Knoop, C. I., & Reavis, C. (1998). *Disney's "The Lion King" (A): The $2 billion movie*. Cambridge, MA: Harvard Business Publishing.

Legal services. (n.d.). Retrieved July 16, 2009, from http://premium.hoovers .com.ezaccess.libraries.psu.edu/subscribe/

Lieberman, M., & Montgomery, D. (1988, Summer). First mover advantages. *Strategic Management Journal, 9*, 41–58.

Liedtka, J. (2006). Is your strategy a duck? *Journal of Business Strategy, 27*(5), 32–37.

luiscar (2008). Gabriela Montero improvises on Mozart's 20 piano concerto [Viewer comment]. Retrieved from: http://www.youtube.com/watch?v=DlZoWUI8 _zg&feature=related

Major, R. (2005, November). It's all about the customer. *Chartered Accountants Journal*, *84*(10), 20–22.

Man in the magic hat. (2001, May 21). *Modern Brewery Age*. Retrieved from http://findarticles.com/p/articles/mi_m3469/is_21_52/ai_75919042/

Maney, K. (2003). *The maverick and his machine*: Thomas Watson, Sr. and the making of IBM. Hoboken, NJ: Wiley.

Mansfield, E. (1986). Patents and innovation: An empirical study. *Management Science*, *32*(2), 173–181.

McCarthy, D., Markides, C., & Mintzberg, H. (2000). View from the top: Henry Mintzberg on strategy and management. *The Academy of Management Executive*, *14*(3), 31–42.

McGahan, A. (2000). How industries evolve. *Business Strategy Review*, *11*(3), 1–16.

McGahan, A. (2004). How industries change. *Harvard Business Review*. *82*(10), 86–94.

McGraw, T. (2009). Driver completion hot as NYC taxi medallions hit $766,000. *USAToday*. Retrieved from http://www.usatoday.com/money/industries/travel/2009-08-05-taxi-cab-new-york-city-medallions_N.htm

Mendelson, H., & Pillai, R. (1999). Industry clockspeed: Measurement and implications. *Manufacturing and Service Operations Management*, *1*(1), 1–20.

Miles, R., & Snow, C. (1978). *Organizational strategy, structure, and process*. New York, NY. McGraw-Hill.

Miles, R., Snow, C., Meyer, A., & Coleman, H., Jr. (1978). Organizational strategy, structure, and process. *Academy of Management Review*, *3*(3), 546–562.

Pew Research Center. *Millennials: Confident. Connected. Open to change*. (2010, February). Retrieved from http://pewsocialtrends.org/assets/pdf/millennials -confident-connected-open-to-change.pdf

Mintzberg, H. (1987a). The strategy concept I: Five Ps for strategy. *California Management Review*, *30*(1), 11–24.

Mintzberg, H. (1987b). The strategy concept II: Another look at why organizations need strategy. *California Management Review*, *30*(1), 25–32.

Mintzberg, H. (1990). The design school: Reconsidering the basic premises of strategic management. *Strategic Management Journal*, *11*(3), 171–195.

Montgomery, C. (1994) *Marks & Spencer, Ltd. (A)*. Cambridge, MA: Harvard Business Publishing.

Montgomery, C. (2008). Putting leadership back into strategy. *Harvard Business Review*, *86*(1), 54–60.

National Aeronautics and Space Administration (NASA). (2007). Learning curve calculator. Retrieved from http://cost.jsc.nasa.gov/learn.html

Neilson, A. (1992). A new metaphor for strategic fit: All that jazz. *Leadership & Organization Development Journal, 13*(5), 3–6.

Nicholls, W. (2008, December 26). Mes amis, we're catching up. *The Washington Post*, p. F8.

O'Reilly, C., & Pfeffer, J. (1995). *Southwest Airlines (A)*. Stanford, CA: The Stanford Graduate School of Business.

Ogle, M. (2006). *Ambitious brew: The story of American beer*. Orlando, FL: Harcourt Books.

Porac, J., & Thomas, H. (1994). Cognitive categorization and subjective rivalry among retailers in a small city. *Journal of Applied Psychology, 79*(1), 54–66.

Porter, M. (1979). How competitive forces shape strategy. *Harvard Business Review, 57*(2), 137–145.

Porter, M. (2008). The five competitive forces that shape strategy. *Harvard Business Review, 86*(1), 78–93.

Porter, M. (1980). *Competitive strategy*. New York, NY: The Free Press.

Porter, M. (1998). Clusters and the new economics of competition. *Harvard Business Review, 76*(6), 77–90.

Ranking of world's top 10 auto groups by sales. (2009). Retrieved from http://www.reuters.com/article/idUST4374320090730

Raspin, P., & Terjesen, S. (2007). Strategy making: What have we learned about forecasting the future? *Business Strategy Series, 8*(2), 116–121.

Reitzes, A. (1995). Gas guzzling: When prices are low at the pumps, who cares about fuel economy? *E: The Environmental Magazine, 6*(4), 26.

Rumelt, R. (1991). How much does industry matter? *Strategic Management Journal, 12*(3), 167–185.

Rumelt, R. (1997). Toward a strategic theory of the firm. In N. J. Foss (Ed.), *Resources, Firms, and strategies: A reader in the resource-based perspective* (pp. 131–145). Oxford University Press.

Rukstad, M., & Collis, D. (2009). *The Walt Disney Company: The entertainment king*. Cambridge, MA: Harvard Business Publishing.

Sabatella, M. (2000). A jazz improvisation primer. Retrieved April 24, 2010 from, http://www.outsideshore.com/primer/primer/ms-primer-3.html

Scherer, F., Beckenstein, A., Kaufer, E., & Murphy, R. (1975). *The economics of multi-plant operations: An international comparisons study*. Cambridge, MA: Harvard University Press.

Schrage, M. (2002). Wal-Mart trumps Moore's law. *Technology Review, 105*(2), 21.

Shapiro, A. (2006). Measuring innovation: Beyond revenue from new products. *Research Technology Management, 49*(6), 42–51.

Singer. J., & Piluso, J. (2009). Five tools to prepare for future discontinuities. *Strategy and Leadership, 38*(1), 17–21.

Snyder, N., & Glueck, W. (1982). Can environmental volatility be measured objectively? *Academy of Management Journal, 25*(1), 185–192.

Sommer, S., Loch, C., & Dong, J. (2009). Managing complexity and unforeseeable uncertainty in startup companies: An empirical study. *Organization Science, 20*(1), 118–133.

Sull, D. (2005). Strategy as active waiting. *Harvard Business Review, 83*(9), 120–129.

Sutton, R. I. (2001). The weird rules of creativity. *Harvard Business Review, 79*(8), 94–103.

Szulanksi, G. (2000). The process of knowledge transfer: A diachronic analysis of stickiness. *Organizational Behavior and Human Decision Processes, 82*(1), 9–27.

Tarsala, M. (2009, July 22). The next blockbuster drugs. *Newsweek*. Retrieved from http://www.newsweek.com/id/207928

Teece, D., Pisano, G., & Shuen, A. (1997). Dynamic capabilities and strategic management. *Strategic Management Journal, 18*(7), 509–533.

Toftoy, C., & Chatterjee, J. (2004). Mission statements and the small business. *Business Strategy Review, 15*(3), 41–44.

Treacy, M., & Wiersema, F. (1993). Customer intimacy and other value disciplines. *Harvard Business Review, 71*(1), 84–93.

Treacy, M., & Wiersema, F. (1995a). *The discipline of market leaders*. Reading, MA: Addison-Wesley Publishing.

Treacy, M., & Wiersema, F. (1995b). How market leaders keep their edge. *Fortune, 131*(2), 88–98.

Tremblay, V., & Tremblay, C. (2005). *The U.S. brewing industry: Data and economic analysis*. Cambridge, MA: The MIT Press.

Update on California auto emissions standards: Auto industry drops *some* of its preemption lawsuits. (Oh, and California finally gets its waiver). [web log post]. (2009, July 6). Retrieved from http://theusconstitution.org/blog.warming/?p=417

U.S. Department of Commerce Bureau of Economic Analysis. (2010). U.S. Economic Accounts. Retrieved March 8, 2010, from http://www.bea.gov/index.htm

U.S. Census Bureau. *U.S. Interim Projections by Age, Sex, Race, and Hispanic Origin: 2000–2050, table 2A*. (2009). Retrieved from http://www.census.gov/population/www/projections/usinterimproj/

U.S. Patent and Trademark Office. (n.d.) *Patent counts by class by year, part A1*. Retrieved from http://www.uspto.gov/web/offices/ac/ido/oeip/taf/cbcby.htm#PartA1-1

Wall, S., & Wall, S. (1995). The evolution (not the death) of strategy. *Organizational Dynamics, 24*(2), 6–19.

Walsh, P. (2005). Dealing with the uncertainties of environmental change by adding scenario planning to the strategy reformulation equation. *Management Decision, 43*(1), 113–122.

Wards Automotive Group. (2010). *U.S. car and truck sales, 1931–2009.* Retrieved from http://wardsauto.com/keydata/historical/UsaSa28summary/

Warner, A., Fairbank, J., & Steensma, H. (2006). Managing uncertainty in a formal standards-based industry: A real options perspective on acquisition timing. *Journal of Management, 32*(2), 279–298.

Warner, A., & Fairbank, J. (2008). Integrating real option and dynamic capabilities theories of firm boundaries: The logic of early acquisition in the ICT industry. *International Journal of IT Standards Research, 6*(1), 39–54.

Wilcox, J. (2010). Will the smartphone replace the PC in three years? Retrieved from http://www.betanews.com/joewilcox/article/Will-the-smartphone-replace-the-PC-in-three-years/1267721779

Williams, S. (1980, July 22). New era: Driving less in smaller cars. *New York Times*, p. B6.

Womack, J., & Jones, D. (1994). From lean production to the lean enterprise. *Harvard Business Review, 72*(2), 93–103.

World Bank. *GDP growth (annual %).* (n.d.). Retrieved from http://datafinder .worldbank.org/gdp-growth-annual

Who said that? (2009). *New Accountant, 732,* 23.

Ying, J. (1990). Regulatory reform and technical change: New evidence of scale economies in trucking. *Southern Economic Journal, 56*(4), 996–1009.

Yoffie, D. (2006). *Cola wars continue: Coke and Pepsi in 2006.* Boston, MA: Harvard Business Publishing.

Zahra, S., & Chaples, S. (1993). Blind spots in competitive analysis. *The Academy of Management Executive, 7*(2), 7–29.

Zahra, S., & Pearce, J., II. (1990). Research evidence on the Miles-Snow typology. *Journal of Management, 16*(4), 751–768.

Index

Note: The *italicized f* and *t* following page numbers refer to figures and tables respectively.